A Teacher's Companion to Essential Motivation in the Classroom

Teachers around the world have found Ian Gilbert's classic text *Essential Motivation in the Classroom* an inspiring and provocative read. This ground-breaking companion to the book is a definitive one-stop guide for teachers who are looking for inspiration as to how his ideas can be put into practice in everyday classrooms. A truly lively and engaging resource, it scrutinises each aspect of Gilbert's now famous 'seven keys' of motivation and provides a wide range of practical ideas, activities and launch pads for discussion which can be blended seamlessly into your own lessons.

Taking as its starting point the right of every child to an inspirational education that develops their values, attitudes and skills, this book provides you with the means to unlock even your most challenging of pupils and will act as a springboard for visionary learning in the classroom and beyond.

Key ideas explored include:

- goal-setting strategies

- students' own intrinsic motivations

- preparing effective challenges

- developing multiple approaches to learning

- using physical activities to anchor learning

- helping students to understand themselves better and be better prepared for the world today.

For teachers of pupils at all ages and stages, this book is easy to follow, easy to 'dip in and out of' and conversational in tone and has the potential to be a game-changer for any teacher wishing to reinvigorate their pupils, colleagues and classrooms.

Georgia Holleran is an educational consultant, working across the curriculum and specialising in combining the worlds of business and education.

Ian Gilbert is an educational innovator, award-winning writer, entrepreneur and inspirational speaker, delivering training to schools and colleges in the UK and worldwide for his 'Independent Thinking' organisation. He has previously published *Essential Motivation in the Classroom* (2012), 2nd edition, and *Why Do I Need a Teacher when I've Got Google?* (2014), 2nd edn, both published by Routledge.

A Teacher's Companion to Essential Motivation in the Classroom

Resources and activities to inspire and engage your students

Georgia Holleran and Ian Gilbert

Routledge
Taylor & Francis Group

LONDON AND NEW YORK

First published 2015
by Routledge
2 Park Square, Milton Park, Abingdon, Oxon OX14 4RN

and by Routledge
711 Third Avenue, New York, NY 10017

*Routledge is an imprint of the Taylor & Francis Group, an informa
business*

British Library Cataloguing in Publication Data
A catalogue record for this book is available from the British Library

Library of Congress Cataloging in Publication Data
Holleran, Georgia.
    A teacher's companion to essential motivation in the classroom :
    resources and activities to inspire and engage your students /
    Georgia Holleran and Ian Gilbert.
        pages cm
    1. Motivation in education—Handbooks, manuals, etc. 2. Academic
    achievement—Handbooks, manuals, etc. I. Gilbert, Ian, 1965– II. Title.
    LB1065.H565 2015
    370.15′4—dc23   2014041919

ISBN: 978-0-415-74860-5 (hbk)
ISBN: 978-0-415-74862-9 (pbk)
ISBN: 978-1-315-79652-9 (ebk)

Typeset in Sabon
by Keystroke, Station Road, Codsall, Wolverhampton

MIX
Paper from
responsible sources
FSC   FSC® C013604
www.fsc.org

Printed and bound by CPI Group (UK) Ltd, Croydon, CR0 4YY

For Mum and Mike

Contents

Foreword

It was my first book. And it took me ages. I had been giving an after-dinner speech in a hotel in Torquay to a group of heads from special schools and Alison Foyle, who was on the lookout for new books to commission, approached me afterwards and asked if I had written a book and would I like to? The answers were: 'No' and 'Yes, very much, where do I sign?'

At that time I was loving the work of American educator Eric Jensen and I had seen his list of seven key factors that help create internally motivated learners. It resonated with my work with young people, helping them get themselves motivated to do well at school and well beyond.

'One sheds one's sicknesses in books' is something D.H. Lawrence once wrote about the writing process. They are also a great way of channelling your thoughts, ideas and passions 'to be master of them', to continue that quotation from Lawrence. *Essential Motivation* allowed me to set down years' worth of reading, talking, thinking and general buzzing in a way that made it all not only manageable but also communicable. What I didn't want to create at that point was a how-to guide with photocopiable worksheets. I didn't want to tell teachers what to do and I still don't. Neither was it meant to be the definitive guide on motivation, hence the late change to the title to include 'Essential' (the essence of). And I definitely wasn't putting out some sort of gospel, hence opening with the quotation I borrowed from Stephen Pinker:

> Every idea in this book may turn out to be wrong, but that would be progress

All I was trying to do was share 'stuff' with teachers that I thought they might find useful.

What I created over a decade ago seems to have touched many, many people, from Geoff Barton's glowing early review for the *TES* to the many teachers and head teachers I meet around the world who talk with such enthusiasm of the book, how their personal copy is dog-eared and full of Post-it Pads and notes in the margin, and how they buy copies for all their new staff each year.

Since its first publication, there have been numerous reprints and even a Spanish translation (*Motivar para aprender en el aula – Las siete claves de al motivación escolar*) which saw numerous e-mails going backwards and forwards between me and the Spanish translator as he tried to make phrases like 'bowling a googly' comprehensible to a Spanish reader. The connection I now have with educators in Chile has proven that it is not only the words that translate but the ideas too, proving the ideas work with some of that country's most troubled young people.

In 2013 I was asked to produce a new edition that allowed me to give the text a bit of a spring clean and update some of the references (apparently Manchester United used to have a manager called 'Alex' something).

It also allowed me to update the dedication, but that's another story.

What I had felt for a while, however, was that a companion book full of practical exercises for teachers might be worthwhile but one – and this was important – *not* written by me. It needed to be written by a real teacher based on their experience in real classrooms and Alison at Routledge agreed. Using the power of Twitter, I then put out a tweet to see if there were any teachers out there who were fans of the book and who felt up to the challenge. Quite a few stepped forward but only Georgia saw it through.

What she has created is exactly what I wanted it to be – a wonderful book in its own right and not simply the colouring book to go with the book of the film in a Disney style. She uses my original seven themes borrowed from Jensen but really sets about making them her own. In doing so, she puts forward a plethora of practical, workable, proven strategies (she is a successful inner-city teacher, after all) that show, despite the current predilection for direct instruction and treating children like buckets both empty and passive in equal measure, this progressive, active, child-centred, touchy-feely stuff actually makes a difference. Of course it does.

I am genuinely thrilled by the success of *Essential Motivation in the Classroom* and even more thrilled with what Georgia has now created to complement it. Please enjoy them both in the spirit with which they were written – fun.

Ian Gilbert
November 2014
Hong Kong

Acknowledgements

So little space, so many people to acknowledge having contributed to my getting to where I am today.

Elaine and Mike Towns, as my mother and step-father, have possibly contributed the most over the years by showing me how to notice, question, pursue and persevere in the name of learning. They continue to this day to discuss and explore all matters under the sun, a model I shall strive to live up to. You could not have been any more perfect parents – thank you.

And at the other end of the spectrum: my adorable daughter Indigo who is my own little social engineering experiment and a delight to witness as she grows and tackles learning about the world for herself. Indigo Pea – long may your extraordinarily bright light shine.

Thanks to those whose support I could not have done without: Meg Khan, the catalyst for so many conversations and insights that have enriched this book a hundredfold and whose company during endless coffee-shop visits has spawned so many amazingly fruitful and exciting projects; Dave and Helena Madgewick whose support and friendship warms through me like sunshine; Jason and Sharon Gale and their truly special ability to make all-comers feel welcome even when up to their eyes in their own creative endeavours; my dear friend and colleague Donald Stavert who put me on the path to Emotional Intelligence all those years back; Irene Simon and Michael Horton who introduced me to NLP even further back; and Martin Holleran: thank you for keeping it real . . .

More specifically connected with this book, I have to start by thanking Ian Gilbert for giving me the opportunity to muck around with his classic *Essential Motivation in the Classroom*; it was an honour and a privilege to be allowed to play around with such amazing raw material. Also Alison Foyle and the team at Routledge who encourage, cheer-lead and support just at the right time and in just the right amounts.

I thank Marion Faust and my friends and colleagues, both past and present, at Newham Education Business Partnership, who allowed me to create anything I wanted to in the name of education and learning. Many activities, visits, games, tours, events and conferences later, I can safely say there was never a dull moment and it was all enormous fun.

Many thanks must also be extended to Chinye Jibunoh of Eastlea Community School, Rachel McGowan of Plashet School and Dame Alison Peacock of The Wroxham School, who have all been wholeheartedly supportive of my efforts to devise engaging activities for their students.

Lastly, thanks to all the people I have had the pleasure of teaching, tutoring, coaching or just gassing with. You really have made all the difference.

Introduction

I want to explain why *you* are my motivation for doing this book.

Causing others to learn stuff is a magic mix of art and science; knowledge is a balance between facts and creativity and the way we learn uses both logic and imagination but the essential factor that cannot be replaced is **you**. Your take on the world comes through everything you do and is the secret to connecting with, and inspiring, the minds of others around you.

Much as we may secretly want to, we cannot simply pull a book off the shelf (or into an online basket) which, with a tweak of a lesson plan, can transform the lost souls in your class into compliant, motivated and focused young citizens of the world. (Actually, you may not want that; I find it a bit 'Midwich Cuckoos' myself.) No book contains the elusive secret or silver bullet that flicks the motivation switch on in those pesky kids. However, *A Teacher's Companion to Essential Motivation in the Classroom* has a trick up its sleeve that ensures that things are done a little differently. And this might not flick a magic switch as such, but may certainly coax a little flame into being. The power of this book is that for it to really work you have to live it yourself. Or in the words of the great man *himself*:

> We cannot separate learning strategies from motivation to learn and also that we look beyond mere strategies to feel for the motivation at attitudinal level. *This is the essence of the 'essential motivation' in the title.* And it means your motivation as well as theirs; after all, the way that you are in the classroom teaches far louder than what you say.
>
> Ian Gilbert, *Essential Motivation in the Classroom*

Writing this book has allowed me to have the pleasure of deeply understanding and distilling Ian's offerings from the original text. The more I understood, the more I knew a book of worksheets, however attractive and popular the idea, would not be the most effective means to put Ian's collected gems into practice. Nor was a book detailing case studies of how School X or Teacher Y managed to get their little darlings tame within one week. Their little darlings are not your little darlings and their school of happy teachers and motivational assemblies may not bear much resemblance to anything you witness on a drizzly Tuesday morning.

Instead, I have constructed this book to allow you to access the wisdom of Ian's original *Essential Motivation in the Classroom* in accessible little chunks that you can sprinkle, blend or otherwise smoosh* into your daily classroom activities. And, while we're on a food-based metaphor: the more you are able to access and use these

---

*Do you *really* need a definition?

delightful ingredients, the better you will become in adjusting their proportions and using their distinctive nuances to flavour your own concoctions. Before you know it, you'll be whipping up gourmet offerings on a BBC reality-based elimination competition and showing us how you can both fall apart and succeed at the same time. Yes, I realise I took the food metaphor just one step too far with that last one, but my point is that the suggestions in this book are but a brief jumping point between the concept of motivation and the reality of life in the classroom. It is a toolkit, a checklist or a handbook (whichever excites you more) of motivation but it needs something else before it can come alive: it needs you to activate it.

So please take what is on offer in these pages and make something extraordinarily and uniquely you with it. Because the 'you' is the magic that brings this whole crazy world of learning alive for our students.

How to use this book

Well, having said all that, I still feel I should give you a bit of a road map. The layout of this book keeps to the format of Ian's original seven chapters, but I've added a few extra bits and bobs towards the end. At the start of each chapter is a brief outline of what's to come, which includes some of Ian's original text that expresses each chapter's essence in the way only he can.

At the end of each chapter you will find the practical materials which you are invited to use in your class, in your school and on yourself. Why yes, you may indeed be the best subject for some of your explorations of motivation. Wouldn't it be great to have the Sunday evening gnaw of trepidation transform into a tingle of excitement? The practical materials come in the form of checklists, outlines of activities and worksheets, designed for use straight from the book or ready for whatever adaptation you see fit to apply.

There is also an additional online resource available at www.routledge.com/cw/holleran where you will find all the direct links to the websites and resources discussed and more, for the insatiably curious. You will also find downloadable versions of all the exercises in this book and a great section of quotes designed to sum up this book's more pithy sentiments. The quotes have many uses, including being casually dropped into conversation or deployed, with added emphasis, when 11R insist they *don't* have any goals; or you can simply print them out as large as possible and plaster your walls for reference on those tricky days when your own motivation may need a boost.

There are also suggestions for how the resources in this book can be used. If you need ideas for collaborative working, whole school policy, self-development or INSET, for example, you can check out the quick reference on page 123. If you are new to much of this content and not sure where to start, you'll find some suggested stages of implementation on page 119. And if you're one of those people who want to start NOW, page 121 has a list of starter basics you can do with little or no preparation that contain the power to transform your classes and, quite crucially, your students' *experience* of your classes.

Motivated for what?

What we'll cover in this chapter:

Making the subject relevant and interesting
Goal-setting strategies
Preparing for the future
Embracing failure

Bad news, I'm afraid. The culmination of six million years' worth of neurological evolution is not the GCSE.

Ian Gilbert, *Essential Motivation in the Classroom*

It's a lovely acronym: WIIFM – or 'What's In It For Me?'. We forget that, as adults, we calculate WIIFM all the time: those extra responsibility points may mean more work but that comes with more pay or, at least, experience in a new field. Undertaking a gruelling fundraising task for charity can be demanding and arduous but lead to an amazing sense of achievement and, of course, funds for the charity. Even deciding what goes in the supermarket trolley is a process of weighing up the gains: hmmm, healthy fruit and veg or a variety of salty snacks to accompany late night TV viewing . . .? But our students don't have any choice in the matter of being in school all day. Don't show up at school and your parents could go to jail is certainly a WIIFM (if only for the parents!). When they are small, our kids go to school because we tell them that's what all kids do and then they realise they get to be with their friends all day. Then, some years later, they hopefully come out with an assortment of qualifications. Well, that was my experience anyway.

It was that feeling of wasting my time at school that got me into teaching in the first place. I felt school could be a lot more useful, particularly for the 'dutiful turn-ups' like me who had no real issue with going in every day but felt like they were just biding their time. When I entered the teaching profession, I wanted to offer students more than that. To me, school should be a place where you are taught the skills to make the most of your amazing life. A place where you learn how to learn. A place where you can build understanding of what you have to offer the world. So, as teachers in the twenty-first century, can we do it? Can we engage the young minds in front of us and ensure their crucial developmental years are fully utilised? That can seem like a tall order when you see them for an hour a week every alternate Thursday. But never fear; inspiring minds is what this chapter is all about.

First, you need to turn into a bit of a marketing guru. Remember what got you into your subject in the first place? If you're a primary teacher, then that's probably because you're fascinated with how young children learn, and for you this section may be a bit more straightforward as many children are often still very much switched on at this age. But if you're a secondary teacher, you may well have a great love or, at the very least, an interest in your chosen subject. Tap into it. You may teach History and only have classes for six weeks at a time on a carousel system, but boy can you make an impact in those six weeks! An impact that could last a lifetime. It is time for you to start infecting others with your enthusiasm.

Pick something you fancy from the list below to start to get a buzz going about your subject both in your classroom and all around school. Remember, what you're trying to do is demonstrate the *benefits* of what your subject offers.

- Find and use great quotes about your subject. Check out this one by Freeman Dyson (no, not *that* Dyson, this one's a really cool physicist and mathematician): 'A good scientist is a person with original ideas. A good engineer is a person who makes a design that works with as few original ideas as possible.'

- Who are the famous people, now and in history, connected to your field?

- What AMAZING things have happened in the world because of your subject?

- Does your subject lead to / support a wide range of jobs? What are the many exciting jobs and careers related to your subject?

- Do you know the various career paths, training and university courses available connected with your subject?

- Reflect on why you find the subject so fascinating. Are you brave enough to be interviewed by your students?

- If you're that way inclined, you could design yourself a marketing campaign aimed at students, teachers and parents. How about a stand at parents' evening . . .?

- What are the ten most fascinating and little-known facts about your subject?

- What's your passion point? Could you make a short presentation or film for assembly?

- Is there any fictional or autobiographical work relating to your subject that you could read aloud that might reveal a different aspect of it? For example, through reading Henry Williamson, I developed an understanding of the realities of the First World War and, of all things, agricultural practices in the 1940s.

- Have you thought of Googling cartoons and illustrations about your subject? Stick 'em up on the walls and in the corridors to inform and entertain queuers, loiterers and visitors.

- Find out the practical, emotional and intellectual issues people have about your subject. How can they be dealt with?

- Are there any false ideas, myths or rumours students hold about your subject that you can prove otherwise?

Activities you can do with your class:

- Make marketing style posters about how brilliant the subject is. Have them around the walls or have a featured poster of the week. Sneak them into other areas of the school.

- Find out what your students like about your subject and why. Promote this.

- Challenge another class scheduled at the same time but studying another subject to a debate about which subject is more useful/relevant/interesting/fun etc.

- Are you brave enough to go head-to-head with another teacher and debate why knowledge of your subject would be more useful for future life? To be performed with panache and humour, no nasty jibes; we're not running for the presidency.

- Generate articles for the school newsletter or school blog or tweet interesting nuggets about your subject out in the real world today.

- Are any of your ex-students studying a subject associated with yours at university or working in a job with subject connections? Use the school alumni, get them in to talk to your classes.

- Keep students updated on news and developments in your subject; this can be via a subject blog or you could start your lessons with something along the lines of 'You'll never guess what happened in geomicrobiology this week'.

If you need to mix it up even more, there's a great *Creativity checklist* in Chapter 7 on page 111, but here are a few key words (and add your own) that, combined with your subject, might spark up an idea or two:

Song	Cartoon	Secret	Competition
TV show	How-to manual	Video	Yes/No
Retro	Enormous	Celebrity	Psychology
Diagram	Lyrics	Timeline	Worldwide
Teach	Drama	Outside	Simplified
Invisible	Extreme	Historical	Amusing

How about:

- Electronics Psychology?

- English How-to manual?

- Retro PE?

- Extreme French?

- Secret Maths?

Well, I could generate ideas like that all day; however, I will stop now as I'm sure you get the idea.

If you excite your students as to the vast, if not endless, possibilities that your subject has to offer, your efforts will cause immeasurable rewards, no exaggeration. By igniting a flicker of interest in your students, you will have created in them Ian's 'Holy Grail' of motivation: internal, or *intrinsic*, motivation, i.e. that which comes from within. It's a self-burning flame from there on in with only occasional fanning needed from you as your students' interests develop. Don't forget this can be just as relevant for younger children too as it is said that 60 per cent of all working scientists developed their interest by the age of 11.

The curriculum wall

Another idea to help promote understanding of your subject within school and do-able at all levels is to make a 'progress chart' of where you are in the curriculum. Bear with me . . .

It came from the quote Ian mentions. Will Smith was talking about what he'd learned from building a brick wall:

> There's nothing insurmountable if you keep laying bricks . . . You go one at a time and eventually there will be a wall . . . I just concentrate on the bricks and the walls take care of themselves.

If Will could see the achievement of building the wall when he looked back on it, we can show our students similar benefits by demonstrating how the individual parts of what we're teaching them build into the whole. Imagine your classroom with a display showing the entire curriculum, term or topic's work from the start to completion. In chunks or 'bricks' to show how the modules of work fit together. This has a lot of uses for your students:

- At the start of the topic/term/year they will be able to see the 'whole' subject. And all that they will be learning in the weeks and months to come.

- Through the duration of the topic/syllabus they will see how all the parts fit together and how the new knowledge builds onto the existing.

- If a student misses any days, the missed work will be easy to identify.

- It's a fantastic visual aid for revision and remembering what to recap when using *The review habit* in Chapter 4 on page 70.

- It's great for those students who like to see the framework of things, as well as those who like to see the details.

- As the days/weeks/months continue, the content and progress through the work will be evident. At the end it could offer an enormous sense of satisfaction for students to see how much they've covered (and hopefully learned!).

The curriculum brick wall could take any form you like, as long as it contains all the elements the students will be studying, in the order you are intending to study them. It could be:

- a colourful snake winding its way around the walls

- a jigsaw to be completed piece by piece

- one of those fundraising 'thermometers' that shows progress climbing up a wall

- advent-calendar style, doors open/close to show topics covered

- just a simple visual of a brick wall showing (paper or card) bricks as they build into the whole topic (If room allows, the bricks could be literally transferred from a pile in one place to build the wall in another.)

- put up on a whiteboard or computer screen, so you can have different walls for different classes.

Each student could have their own personal copy, not as a list though; what we're attempting to do here is to show how the bricks build into the complete wall.

There are probably 101 more ways to present this information; I expect Tracy Emin would make a quilt out it. You could ask your students how it could be meaningfully presented to them and then get several different representations according to what students prefer. This is a great method to illustrate a body of knowledge, which can come in handy during revision and exams as students learn to map each subject to show all the topics to be covered.

So now we have your students all fired up about your subject and what they are going to learn, let's see where it ties in with what *they* want.

We'll start with Ian's great *Wish list* exercise on page 16 where students can day-dream about their future. Another way you can get your students to think about what they want is to ask them what makes them happy; see worksheet *What makes you happy?* on page 17. Being good at something is not the same as liking it. I have lost count of how many Masterchef contestants have successful careers as doctors, architects, accountants and such like, yet are yearning to open their own restaurant or work in a professional kitchen. And, by the looks of it, you'd really have to *love* working in a professional kitchen to survive the pressure. And the head chef.

There is also *Design a world where anything is possible* on page 18. Younger students will also enjoy the activities about future worlds on the Literacy Shed website. Search for it or find details in the online resources. Encourage students to let their imaginations go wild. After all, are you old enough to remember when phone numbers were attached to a property, not a person? Do you remember seeing a film at the cinema and then waiting years before it came on TV? (And then you missed it if you were out!) I remember watching *Hitchhiker's Guide to the Galaxy* on TV in the early 1980s, based on the book by the amazingly far-sighted Douglas Adams. In it, one of our heroes, Ford Prefect (yes, read the book!), bases his travels on a device which has a small screen and keyboard and fits in the palm of his hand. Ford typed in what he wanted to know and his guide told him all the information he needed in the entire universe. Sound familiar? The wonderful Douglas Adams had predicted the smart-phone in a time when computers were still rare in the home, 'mobile' phones worked through your car (and only if you were rich!) and the internet was only a messaging service between some American universities. So get your students to let rip and see what's in store for all our futures.

The world is full of material that we take for granted today which someone somewhere was once told was impossible. Roger Bannister was told that if he ran that fast, his heart would burst. Chuck Yeager was told that if he tried to fly through the sound barrier, the vibrations would lead to the disintegration of his craft. In 1865 *The Boston Post* declared that: 'Well informed people know that it is impossible to transmit the voice over wires and that were it possible to do so, the thing would be of no practical value.' I find no record of the reliability of the tips on their racing pages. Aerodynamically speaking, bees cannot fly. It's just that they don't know it. Scientifically speaking, a pike should not be able to accelerate as fast as a NASA rocket, that is to say at twelve times the force of gravity. So, don't tell it.

Ian Gilbert, *Essential Motivation in the Classroom*

If you're looking ahead long-term, and what you see looks like science fiction, it might be wrong. But if it doesn't look like science fiction, it's definitely wrong.

Christine L. Peterson, president of the Foresight Institute

When your students have got it all sorted and the future wrapped up, get them to tell you all about it by:

- writing a story

- writing a future newspaper report or diary entry

- taking the role of a news reporter at the scene of a new product launch

- drawing their ideas

- devising a short play or assembly to explain their idea

- designing a technical manual to show how an idea works

- voting for the idea most likely to happen

- voting for the most innovative/exciting idea

- researching the technology needed

- investigating the internet to see if other people have had a similar idea

- researching a suitable organisation and writing an enquiry letter to ask about the feasibility of their idea happening.

With younger children you can also get them thinking a bit more about their future by asking them what they think they'll be doing aged 20 or 25. Some children struggle with seeing so far into their own future (what with 25 being positively *ancient*!) but some are quite specific as to where they are going and what they want to be. If you like using guided visualisation, you can get the class to close their eyes while you talk them through a script about their future life. There's a sample script, *Visualise your future*, on page 19 and a follow-up activity, *Capturing the dream*, on page 20. After this activity encourage the students to talk about their thoughts:

- Ask how many of them owned their own business, had a flash car or had their own house or flat? What implications does this have about the amount of money they must be earning?

- Were they using interests and skills they are already developing?

- Were they happy with their chosen daydream, or could they now improve or change it in some way?

- What did they learn about themselves during this activity?

Another useful exercise is to *Make a vision board* (page 21). A vision board is a collection of images (and sometimes words) made to describe an individual's hopes and aspirations. Search for 'vision boards' or 'kids vision boards' in Google images to see loads of examples. It can be started and then built upon over days and weeks to get it just right and then either pinned up somewhere for daily inspiration or tucked away and forgotten about, until happening across it many years later causing shock as to how many images have 'come true'. (If we ever meet, ask me to tell you my vision board story – it's a good one!) Using the technique of collecting images or imagining something sends very powerful messages to the brain. It's like giving a sniffer dog the scent of contraband and letting it loose on the luggage carousel. By giving the brain clear messages as to what is wanted, it can then set about making it happen either consciously or subconsciously.

After building themselves a picture of what they want, your students can start to piece together a simple plan of action. If you get a child who, for example, wants to be a daredevil stunt-bike rider, get them to tell you what they did before (*just before*) they succeeded in being a daredevil stunt-bike rider. And then what they did before that. Some children are brilliant at being able to tell you their whole career path, stepping right back to the school they are in today. Sooner or later the phrase 'well to do that I just made loads of money', or something similar, comes up. Yep, it is pretty useful for most people to have 'make money' somewhere on their plan for the future. This line of thought can be explored in many ways:

- Will they get a job / become self-employed / start a business?
- What will they be doing?
- What qualifications are required?
- What experience is needed?
- Where will they study?
- Where will they train?
- How are they going to start?
- What will be their annual income?
- Who else will be involved?

Start finding some answers to these questions and your students will be well on their way to making a working plan of action. The point of the exercise is to get them to start thinking about what they want in life and showing them a simple thought process to develop their dreams and ideas into goals and a tangible plan. And it works for all aspects of life – not just jobs and careers. I met one fab Year 5 girl who wanted to have a family with lots of babies by the time she was 25 (her dream, I'm not going to judge!). After we got chatting about the expense of having all those children, she decided she needed a rich husband to help her with them. It wasn't long before she decided she had better marry a footballer and a minute later she was planning to train in sports massage (or Soft Tissue Therapy as it would like to be known) because that way you get to meet a lot of footballers. Greatly relieved that she wasn't planning on meeting a footballer by falling over him drunk in a 'Top West End Club', I was also surprised and impressed by her realistic approach. Time will tell whether my little friend gets her dream of babies via footballers and soft tissue manipulation, but at least she now had a plan. And, more importantly, she has the rudimentary skills to make a plan or – er – change this one if she ever wanted to. Because, of course, the next thing I mention is that because this is their plan they can adapt it and change it as their circumstances or ideas change. The point is to have a plan, but not to stick rigidly to it if it no longer inspires you as you evolve over the years.

You can also look at the answers to *The wish list* and *What makes you happy?* and connect them to Gardner's multiple intelligences, covered in Chapter 2. The connections and patterns might cause a few insights. It is important to let students know their answers to these types of questions will evolve and change over the years, so they should be encouraged to do them to reveal more of a snapshot of what they are about, not a fixed judgement of their capabilities. And with older students, and adults too, **no diagnostic should be taken as unshakable fact** but treated with more of a 'hmmm, that's interesting' approach.

And while we're on the subject, notice how I have brought the conversation neatly round to people knowing themselves? Well, guess what? You too can do all these exercises and take a bit of time to think about what makes *you* happy. The real key to getting your students to understand the value of these exercises is to have walked the talk and seen its value for yourself. Your authentic explanations will demonstrate that you value the notion of understanding yourself, and your students will be intrigued to try it for themselves. It also works to call this knowledge 'secrets', as in 'Want to know the secret for getting the most brilliant job in the world?' or 'Who wants to know the secret to owning a Ferrari/beach house/zoo?'. Works every time.

So before you start getting your students to examine their dreams, what are yours? DO you still have dreams? Are you aiming for what you want in life? And, more to the point, if your dreams are not matching your reality, don't you think it's time to do something about it?

I am a big fan of looking after Number One. Namely me. Now don't get me wrong, I have family and I am surrounded by people I love so of course I care for them all too, but I've learned that if I'm OK then I'm in better shape to attend to their needs. Put it simply: I'm more use to them if I am coming from a happy place. It's the aeroplane journey with children analogy so often used: if the cabin pressure drops and the oxygen masks appear, put yours on first, then tend to the others. How many times do we see the opposite in action, with teachers and parents running on empty?

It's the same in the classroom. If you're a generally happy chappy going about your business, getting on with life, making goals and doing a bit of teaching here and there, then you are modelling a great example of an adult living life to the full. If, however, you are stuck in a rut and bored or frustrated, then it will be hard for you to encourage your students to dream big and plan for success.

So, need more encouragement than simply filling in a worksheet? Well, there are some brilliant people out there on the web who have books, courses, blogs and all sorts of resources to help you find your source of inspiration: Marianne Cantwell, Ramit Sethi, John Williams, the guys at Escape the City, Barbara Sher and Tim Ferris, for example. I have personally experienced all these people's offerings and I can recommend their approaches (otherwise I wouldn't have put you on to them). I have no affiliation links or anything with them; I just like what they have to say and how they say it. Have a search for them and maybe one will strike a chord with you. For direct links to their websites see the online resources.

If it looks like I'm suggesting that part of the getting inspired process includes finding something else to do other than teaching, you couldn't be further from the truth. What I am encouraging you to do is to be inspired and therefore be an inspir-*ing* person. Go all out to discover what truly makes you light up and make strides towards it. If that means you leave your post in two years' time because you've set up a riding school for youngsters who use wheelchairs, then you truly have my blessing. If you find you're more motivated in the classroom because you've finally started your novel on the side, then I'm chuffed for you. If you discover that you're secretly completely in love with education and harbouring a desire to start your own school, then I couldn't be happier.

You see I believe that because you have been inspired to become a teacher at some point in your life, then you never really leave the profession behind, no matter where you go. The desire to share your knowledge and encourage others remains as a driving force throughout your life. And if you do leave your mainstream teaching role to be a photojournalist visiting the war-torn countries of this world, then make a date to come back and tell your former students all about it. Or run an after-school club or a special course or a summer school. Kids need you to inspire them. So make a point of doing an investigative number on yourself and become inspired.

Goal setting

So once we have got our students all fired up and inspired, it's time to introduce them to a process whereby they can actually make their dreams come true. No this is not a Disney movie, it's time for the cold hard facts about goal setting. Get ready for some great and oh-so-true quotes:

> I have not come across an individual doing extraordinary things in any walk of life who did not use goal setting, in some form or another.
>
> Ian Gilbert, world expert in thinking skills

> It's the thinking that goes into the writing, not the words that end up on the paper, that makes the difference.
>
> Tom Monaghan, founder of Domino's Pizza

> By recording your dreams and goals on paper, you set in motion the process of becoming the person you most want to be. Put your future in good hands – your own.
>
> Mark Victor Hansen, author and motivation guru.

Hopefully, even if they don't wholeheartedly believe you when you say how important goal setting is, your students will one day run up to you in the street and engulf you in a huge bear hug. Ideally because they took your advice to heart, made some ambitious goals, caused them to happen and now reside on a paradise island; rather than because they ignored your advice, didn't make any goals and are now destitute and need to crash on your couch 'for a few days'.

> There is the story, regularly rolled out to confirm the power of goal setting, regarding the survey of students at Yale University in the 1930s. In among a whole host of questions designed to draw a picture of the young, upwardly mobile American of the time was a question asking the respondent whether he or she had *written* goals with plans for their achievement. Only a handful did. Thirty years later, so the story goes, the University followed up to see just what they had achieved. What they discovered was that students who had written goals were all happy and successful in a number of ways, were all financially independent and were all worth more individually than the *rest of the students put together*.
>
> Ian Gilbert, *Essential Motivation in the Classroom*

OK, so we know goal setting is important (and don't for one minute think **you're** going to get away with not making any) so what constitutes an effective strategy? For one thing you may have heard of the SMART acronym, with each letter standing for . . .

- specific

- measurable/motivational

- achievable/action-orientated/aimed/accountable

- relevant/realistic/responsible

- timely/time-bound/touchable.

. . . depending on which guru you consult.

It doesn't matter which version you use because . . . I don't know about you but I find as soon as I have to consider whether my dreams are achievable and relevant, all the magic starts to evaporate. So let's start with the fundamentals of goal setting and the only word in the SMART acronym that's always the same: specific.

Hopefully enough ideas been generated from the activities above to help everyone come up with at least one specific goal. As much time as needed can be taken at this stage as it is important that the goal stated is personally relevant and inspiring. Because there's no sense in making a goal that is not personally inspiring or that is more of a vague maybe. Or that might actually be somebody else's goal in disguise . . .

> Don't ask yourself what the world needs. Ask yourself what makes you come alive and then go do that. Because what the world needs is people who have come alive.
>
> Howard Thurman, author, philosopher and civil rights leader.

And yes, even if the student doesn't appear to have any ideas for a goal, it is worth looking again at *The wish list* and *What makes you happy?* exercises because time moves on and we're all heading somewhere whether it is planned or not! I won't pile in loads of 'If you don't have a map of where you want to go, you'll end somewhere else' quotes but goals can definitely be lifestyle rather than career related. As Edward, a little four-year-old friend of mine, recently said, 'I want to be a train driver AND a father.'

For students with their goals firmly in mind try the worksheet *I can see into the future* on page 22, and *Goal setting made simple* on page 23 kicks off the tying the goals down process nicely. *Goal setting made simple* is particularly good as it allows you to follow the process that computer scientists Allen Newell and Herbert Simon define as intelligence: 'specifying a goal, assessing the current situation to see how it differs from the goal, and applying a set of operations to reduce the difference'. Bearing in mind they were studying artificial intelligence, we can learn a lot by applying this logical process to realising our goals. I think Mr Spock would approve. There is more about this process in Chapter 4.

But enough of all this talk of goal setting and fantastic futures, let's get back to reality: having dreams and making plans are all very well but it can't work out for everyone all the time can it? We tell our students they can dream anything and then make it happen but what about when they fail and realise they can't have what they want? What are they supposed to do then?

Was that a little voice in your head talking? This type of response is from someone who doesn't fully see the power behind aiming high and going for dreams. Of course the dreams are the incentive and achieving them is the prize, but what you *gain* is what you learn and who you become along the way. Now before you start looking at me sideways and thinking that statement was a bit 'new age', you surely have to admit that I might have a point. Our experiences challenge and change us throughout our whole lives, and that can be the case right the way into old age. Somewhere along the line a thing called wisdom kicks in and we tend to make fewer of the same mistakes, but the experiences we've lived through make us who we are.

Easy? Apparently not. If the goals identified are personally meaningful and the experience of achieving them would be brilliant, surely everyone with goals would be doing nothing but using every minute of their every day to work towards them. So why then do people avoid setting goals or avoid working on these goals once identified? You see the thing is people like to *think* of their goals but taking the steps proves a bit trickier. And if it's stopping people the world over, you can be sure it will be stopping your students somewhere along the line. Let's give it a name: FEAR.

And it can get in the way of **everything**.

Have you heard of Susan Jeffers' best-selling book *Feel the Fear and Do It Anyway*? Well, you don't have to read the whole book to benefit from its message because the gist is in the title, with emphasis on DO IT ANYWAY. Do you think your students are alone in being halted from progress by fear? Nope. Do people live with fear but get on with their goals anyway? Yep.

Here's a great quote from the lovely singer Adele, but perhaps not one to pop up on the wall or read if you're having your lunch right now:

> I'm scared of audiences. One show in Amsterdam I was so nervous, I escaped out the fire exit. I've thrown up a couple of times. Once in Brussels, I projectile vomited on someone. I just gotta bear it. But I don't like touring. I have anxiety attacks a lot.

Or, I completely love this by Hugh Jackman:

> The most scared I'd ever been was the first time I sang at a rugby match, Australia versus New Zealand, in front of one hundred thousand people. I had a panic attack the night before because people have been booed off and never worked again . . . just singing one song, the national anthem.

Oh go on then. Just one more:

> A lot of people ask me when I do a stunt, 'Jackie, are you scared?' Of course I'm scared. I'm not Superman.

That last one from the wonderful Jackie Chan. And all these people use performance as a way to make a living. However, all *we're* talking about here is your students taking steps towards something they dream of doing. Perspective people please!

OK, so Fear of Failure, we all suffer from it. Want to know what can be done about it?

Please stop reading now, grab your internet-able device and search: Art Williams 1987.

Art Williams was a former high-school football coach who changed careers as a result of his father's death and the family discovering they were woefully underinsured. His astonishingly successful and innovative style of management is now legendary. Grab a cup of tea, relax and watch the whole speech if you can; it's around 20 minutes long and worth every minute.

If you're not inspired after that, then close this book now. Today's not your day.

However, if Art has encouraged you to 'do it' (please hear the southern drawl), I challenge you and your students to be some of the rare people that actually DO do it. Because the vast majority of people, however many times they hear motivational speeches, take motivational courses and read books entitled *Essential Motivation in the Classroom*, will still fail to actually DO the doing bit!

I don't know if the disclosure laws are different in Australia, but I was reading about an e-course being offered by an Australian company and found their amazing disclaimer clause at the end of their online offering. Words to the effect of: Don't blame us if you buy this course and don't take action. A certain percentage of people will buy this course and not take action and that percentage is in the region of 85 per cent (!).

So I implore you to encourage your students to be among the few and buck the trend. Inspire them to be one of the 15 per cent (or whatever) that makes a plan and then actually does it.

> Twenty years from now you will be more disappointed by the things you didn't do, than by the things that you did do.
>
> Attributed to the best-selling author H. Jackson Brown's mother

Actually I can give you another tip to help your students to be among the few who take action on their goals. How about we all agree that they can start their plan and take the steps, but they don't have to get any of the steps right? They just do them, as Art Williams says. It doesn't matter if the steps work out or not. No one's looking, it's fine.

Ahem, there is a lot of genius in this idea. According to research, the brain loves to complete things so if your students are procrastinating and putting something off, encourage them to just get it under way somehow. Because, if they actually start it, their brains will file it under 'incomplete' and therefore they are more likely to come back to complete it. And we all know the very thing we have been putting off is never *that* bad once we get it under way. The other genius aspect of just starting goals in this way is that by taking steps towards a goal, even if they don't work out as planned, each step taken is adding to that person's knowledge and experience.

> Failure is simply the opportunity to begin again, this time more intelligently.
>
> Henry Ford

Well said. And such a positive attitude towards failure is of paramount importance. I may have to say that again. *A positive attitude towards failure is of paramount importance.*

Experiencing failure is actually necessary and I'll go as far as to say *vital* for our young people to succeed.

Time for Ian's great sunflower story:

> My daughter once brought a sunflower home from her primary school, which we looked after and protected, tying it to the trelliswork on the wall as it grew. We were amazed at how it grew, a thick, straight stem, almost two inches in diameter, rising to a height of around fifteen or sixteen feet. We were both impressed with the result of our loving handiwork. A couple of weeks later we had a storm. In the morning we found the sunflower lying across the path like a felled tree. The tears went on for weeks until my daughter finally managed to get me to stop crying. Nearby, a pensioner had planted a veritable hedge of sunflowers that were neither staked nor tied to the wall and would flap about in the wind like a row of deliboppas in what I thought was a laughable way, yet after the storm all of these sunflowers were still standing.
>
> Ian Gilbert, *Essential Motivation in the Classroom*

By experiencing and understanding failure, young people can build resilience and understand how to *handle* failure. No matter how successful they are at school young people still need to develop resilience to help them overcome future disappointments and challenging situations, like those upstanding sunflowers. Gradually your students should become more comfortable with the concept of failure. Always be sure to stress it is not *them* that is failing, but the *approach* they chose to take at that time. A great response to failure is to say: 'Oh OK, that didn't work then.' Then to get up, dust off and get back on with it.

I mean if we all stopped at the first or 100th sign of failure, we wouldn't be walking, talking, riding bikes, driving cars, falling in love, being voted into power or taking penalties in front of a world audience.

So an acknowledgement that failure is part of the process of success may help some young people relax and start on their goals. Perhaps even looking out for the failures shows them that they're making progress. The exercise *Reflection on failure*, page 74, might also be useful. There's lots more to do with constructive failure on Chapter 4. But right now let's not dwell on failure; go forth and inspire, inspire, inspire. And don't forget to have some deliciously exciting goals of your own:

Dream lofty dreams, and as you dream, so you shall become. Your vision is the promise of what you shall one day be; your ideal is the prophecy of what you shall at last unveil.

James Allen, *As a Man Thinketh*

The wish list

1. If the world were to end in 12 months, which five places would you visit before it did?

2. Somebody has invented a magic 'success' potion. Having taken the potion, no matter what you do, you will succeed. What five things would you do if you knew you could not fail?

3. It is International Work Experience Week, and you can try any job in the world. Which five would you try first?

4. You have been elected President of the World! What five things would you introduce to make the world a better place for everybody in it?

5. You have a magic pen. Whatever you write comes true. The magic only lasts for three minutes. Quickly write down your plans for the next five years. Include qualifications, further education, year-off plans, hobbies you want to try, people you want to meet, places you want to go to, etc. . . .

After answering all the questions think back to what you have discovered.

Which question was the easiest to answer? Why?
Which was the hardest? Why?
Did any of your answers surprise you? Why?
What were the themes that came out in your answers?
What new ideas have you got from doing this exercise?
What is going to change as a result of doing this exercise?

  © 2015 *A Teacher's Companion to Essential Motivation in the Classroom*, Georgia Holleran and Ian Gilbert, Routledge

What makes you happy?

Write a list of all the things that make you feel happy. Simply that.

Don't censor your list. If knowing that your little brother is away all afternoon at a friend's house makes you happy, then write it down. If daydreaming and staring out of the window makes you happy, include that too. You get the idea.

Take some time to build this list as you will probably have more ideas pop into your head if you mull for a bit.

When you have a list of things that make you happy, take some time to see if there are any connections or patterns:

What connections can you make between the things that make you happy?

E.g. You're with a group of people, you're outside, you're building something, etc.

When you are imagining the things that make you happy, what do you notice? Do you see them, hear them, smell, taste or touch them?

When thinking about things that make you happy, are you remembering real events or imagining new ones?

How can you make sure you do more of the things that make you happy?

Design a world where anything is possible

Work on your own or with someone else to describe a future world where anything is possible. Here are some questions you can answer if you get a bit stuck:

- What will everyday life be like?

- What will have been invented?

- What will we no longer use?

- What will we do for entertainment?

- How will we travel?

- What will schools be like?

- What will we do on holiday?

Visualise your future

*Read the following slowly and clearly to the class; * denotes a good pause between sentences to allow time for thinking.*

Now all you need to do is get comfortable, close your eyes and get ready to dream about your future. I'll give you a few seconds now to get comfy and relaxed and then we'll start.
*

Imagine what you would like your life to be like in ten years' time (or whatever is appropriate) when you are grown up.
*

Now it is morning and you have just woken up. What do you see? What can you hear? What can you smell or touch?
*

You get up and start to get dressed. What clothes do you see in your wardrobe? What will you choose to wear for work today?
*

You are now eating breakfast. Where are you? What can you see? Hear? Smell? Taste?
*

Time has passed and you're getting ready and leaving for work. Where do you go for your work? How do you travel there?
*

When you arrive at your workplace, who do you see there? What are they doing? What can you hear? What do you notice?
*

As you get down to your work, what is the first thing you need to do today? How do you feel about your work?
*

Take a few seconds now to see the kinds of work you do. Are you busy today? What do you do at lunchtime? What can you see? What can you hear? Where are you?
*

You are nearing the end of your day. What is the last thing you need to do before leaving work? What time do you leave?
*

Where are you going to go now that your work has finished?
*

Take a few minutes now to review your day.
*

How did you feel about it?
*

What were the most important or easy to imagine parts of it?
*

Did you have any ideas or notice anything in particular that was important to you?
*

Now in the next few minutes come slowly back into the room and open your eyes. Stay thinking about what you have experienced.
-END-

Capturing the dream

Take some time to note down your main thoughts and ideas that have come from your daydream about the future.

In particular:

- What do you think are the most important feelings you had about your day?

- What sort of environment did you live in? Were you in the city? Countryside? Another country?

- What sort of work were you doing? Were you working with people, ideas or things mainly?

- Did you use any skills or interests that you have now?

- Was it your business, or did you work for someone else?

- Did you like the work you chose for yourself? Explain your answer.

Make a vision board

This works brilliantly with both children and adults. If you are doing this with a whole class, encourage them to start bringing in magazines for a few weeks before you run the exercise.

You will need:

- Large sheets of blank paper or smaller sheets to tape together as the ideas grow!

- Lots of magazines. The glossy ones are the best but also useful are travel brochures, catalogues, old calendars, promotional material, etc.

- Scissors and glue.

Tell everyone they are going to look for pictures that attract them in some way. It could be anything they like: a thing, a place, a person, a lifestyle, colours and shapes, words that inspire them, whatever they want.

It can be tricky to manage a class sharing magazines but stress the importance of them taking the picture they want and then letting the magazine go. If you have one picture of a sunny beach, you don't need three others!

After picture collecting has been going on a while, encourage everyone to start to sort their images and see if any patterns are emerging. Maybe they have found lots of pictures of animals, or houses, or cars. Perhaps there is a lot of travel indicated. Or clothes and fashion.

When they are ready, your students can start to stick down their images. They can do this in whatever way is meaningful to them. Some people like to group their images together or have them make up a whole picture of some sort. It is entirely up to them. Extra paper can be added to make bigger sheets if necessary.

As the exercise progresses, more pictures can be added until the magazine supply has been exhausted or the time has run out.

As the session ends, ask your students:

- Are there any images they would like to have on their sheet but couldn't find?

- If so, where could they look to find them and stick on later?

- When the vision board is finished, what do they intend to do with it?

  - Put it somewhere it will inspire them every day.

  - Keep collecting and adding images.

  - Tuck it away somewhere and make a note to look at it in five years' time!

Finally, remind your students to put today's date on their vision board. It really is surprising to look at old vision boards like this and see how much 'came true'.

I can see into the future . . .

Three Ps of goal -setting:

- **Personal** – has meaning for you.

- **Present tense** – as if it's happening today.

- **Positive** – something you want.

Bearing these in mind, what will you be doing in two years' time?

I am
(e.g. I am studying three A levels at Midtown VI Form or I am an apprentice at Pet Groom salon)

I got there by:
(What are the exams you are currently taking and what grades do you need to get you where you want to go? Don't forget to mention any relevant work experience, interviews or extra courses that are needed too!)

Now take this sheet and pin it somewhere you will see it every day.

Goal setting made simple

Step 1 – What do you want? (*Be specific*)

Step 2 – When do I want it? (*Give it a deadline*)

Step 3 – What do you have to do? (*List the steps you need to take, then START!*)

Step 4 – Check and re-check (*Is it working out the way you want? If no, then how can you get back on course?*)

Enjoy the journey

Goal setting is useful and can get you where you want to be – but don't forget about living now, today! Don't spend all your life looking into the future . . .

Go with the flow

What we'll cover in this chapter:

Working with challenges, deadlines and targets
Multiple intelligences
The primacy/recency effect
Divergent thinking

> You may be the only person in a child's life who is passionate about anything so it is up to you to teach them – by example – how much can be achieved with passion.
>
> Ian Gilbert, *Essential Motivation in the Classroom*

OK, so next up is something fairly crucial to having a successful career. And, perhaps more importantly, absolutely VITAL to having a happy life. I'll put it simply: knowing yourself. In this chapter we're going to look at ways your students can learn to understand themselves a bit better. And by that I don't mean just noticing how they do stuff, but actually finding out specific things about themselves, understanding how they operate under stress, how they attempt to solve problems, what the best working rhythm is for them, etc.

It all pays off because, for example, if a student knows that they work great under pressure, enjoy the outdoor life and have lots of energy, but need to make sure they eat every three to four hours to keep their energy up, they might be better suited to a sporting environment or landscaping and grounds maintenance rather than, say, a city-based call centre. However, if another student is self-driven, enjoys connecting with people and likes the challenge of hitting earnings targets, the call centre environment may well be a perfect match. Obviously it is not quite as simple as that but I find it amazing how many people are sat in jobs they either do not enjoy or have undergone years of training to get and then feel they can't leave. This IS our one and only life and it's never too late to wake up and decide that today is the day when we do what *we* want to do.

And so wouldn't it be brilliant to have this awareness developed during school so that a student always had a mind to where their best strengths and interests lay? Passing exams is certainly a skill, and a celebrated one, but not one that is often needed outside in the world of work. So often the many additional (and largely 'unexamined') skills that people have are ignored or marginalised as the exam years loom into view. Sadly, while these skills are being ignored, the people who own them are thinking that they aren't as important. I have lost count of the number of times I have heard grown adults tell me they 'couldn't do maths' yet they run their own businesses and family happily budgeting, calculating and estimating without breaking a sweat.

Then there was the guy I knew who referred to himself as 'thick' because he failed his eleven plus, who actually very capably headed up accounts at the UK headquarters of a huge telecoms firm. And the woman I met who 'wasn't the clever one' so she stayed living at home to look after dad, yet was also a senior manager in a key department in her workplace with over a dozen staff reporting to her. The impressions we receive about ourselves in childhood stay with us for life, unless we take time to unpick them and see them for what they are: merely other people's opinions. Not fact.

Which is why we must spend some time allowing our young students to discover their strengths and all their interests and capabilities. Some, of course, relating directly to the curriculum upon which they will be tested, and some which might be their utter joy and path to riches one day.

The main part of this chapter will be centred on cultivating that lovely sense of learning when we don't even think we're learning, or as Mihaly Csikszentmihalyi (pronounced Me-high Chick-SENT-me-high, impress your friends) succinctly refers to it: flow. Flow is at its most evident when we have a high challenge but low sense of stress about it. This idea took a while for me to fully comprehend but I got it when I was watching my daughter learn to ride her bike. She would sit on her bike walking herself along and lifting her feet to take a hasty push at a pedal every now and then. Then she'd find she could push the pedals twice round. Then three pushes, or maybe back to one and build up again. She must have spent hours absorbed in what she was trying to achieve until she got the balance right, got the movements right, everything came together and she found she could ride without fiercely concentrating on it. So I came to understand that flow could also be found when we're so keen to achieve something that the 'practice' doesn't feel like practice at all but actually part of the pleasure.

Now wouldn't it be great if school was even sometimes like that for all our students? Notice I said *all* our students. Even the ones who are longing to be outside and climbing a tree. If part of school life caused students to feel moments of flow and those moments were brought to their attention ('Karl, I see you've cleaned out the guinea pigs three times already this week. You're really in flow when it's your turn to look after them, aren't you!') then perhaps more students would feel more able more often.

So the feeling of being more able more often is what we're after. And one of the first things you can do to help your students feel more able more often is to introduce to them Howard Gardner's multiple intelligence theory. This is the one where Howard Gardner identified eight different sorts of intelligences that people have and the special attributes of each one.

The original labels are sometimes adjusted to help people understand their definitions a bit more, which might be useful when introducing your students to this concept:

Gardner's identified intelligence	Label modified for easier understanding
Linguistic Intelligence	Word Smart
Logical-Mathematical Intelligence	Logic Smart
Musical Intelligence	Music Smart
Bodily-Kinaesthetic Intelligence	Body Smart
Spatial Intelligence	Picture Smart
Interpersonal Intelligence	People Smart
Intrapersonal Intelligence	Self Smart
Naturalist Intelligence	Nature Smart

Before we go any further, and as I've mentioned before, it is in no way helpful for a young person to identify with one or more of the intelligences and then think that's that. What Gardner is doing here is not only demonstrating the different ways in which we are intelligent but also that there are different ways to *be* intelligent. So, for example, if you discover you have special aptitudes for spatial, musical and naturalist intelligence, by all means investigate these avenues but don't let that knowledge stop you developing skills in the other intelligences too. Even better, by identifying that you have a specific skill in, say, musical intelligence, you can use that skill to help develop other intelligences by perhaps writing your own lyrics (Linguistic), learning how to read music (Logical-Mathematical) or designing your own choreography (Bodily-Kinaesthetic).

As for the identification of the individual intelligences, I would say that is more of an art than a science. There are numerous tests and quizzes to be found if you search online and it only takes a few minutes to track down one, answer the questions and, bingo, there's your 'score'. If you want a quick one to print out and use with your students, then see *Gardner's intelligences quick quiz* on pages 34–35. However, I think exploration and identification of the different intelligences can be done in other ways with, perhaps, more accuracy and certainly a more thorough understanding of the process.

The first way I would suggest introducing the idea of multiple intelligences would be to discuss with your students what each of the intelligences is; see *Gardner's multiple intelligences descriptors* on pages 36–40, and see if they can come up with people, either real or fictional, who fit each of the criteria. There is also an exercise *Who's who* on page 41 that matches a person with a possible intelligence attribute.

Once your students have got the idea about multiple intelligences, then they might start to identify with one or two of them. This is a very important stage in their understanding of themselves and it is vital that two points are stressed:

1. At this age students are identifying their *natural* intelligences, those that come to them without effort. This does not mean they cannot or will not develop other intelligences.

2. All intelligences are equally important and valuable in the world. Stress that the school environment currently only develops and tests three or four of the intelligences.

Your overall aim of introducing the idea of multiple intelligences is to help students who are concerned that they are different or stupid understand that they have their own intelligences and that those intelligences are just as valid. By working with a student's own identified intelligences, they can then begin to build up the ones they are less naturally able in. Whenever this concept is introduced, most people immediately think of an example similar to this: a (Naturalist) kid who is only interested in fishing can be encouraged to read and write (Linguistic) more about his prized fish. But of course it works brilliantly all throughout the intelligences. Sometimes a little peek into the future can help spark an interest:

Natural intelligence	+	Developed intelligence	=	Possible outcome
Musical	+	Logical-Mathematical	=	running own record label
Intrapersonal	+	Linguistic	=	self-help blogger
Bodily-Kinaesthetic	+	Naturalist	=	outdoor challenge designer

Spatial	+	Musical	=	West End producer
Logical-Mathematical	+	Interpersonal	=	TV quiz show inventor
Linguistic	+	Spatial	=	architectural critic
Interpersonal	+	Bodily-Kinaesthetic	=	interactive exhibit curator

OK, stop me now.

Another thing you can do to spot the different intelligences in your classes is to vary your teaching approach across the intelligence spectrum and observe who thrives and who is out of their depth with each task. There's a *Brilliant intelligences activities list* on pages 42–45 to help you decide what to inflict upon them. Another interesting way to see your classes' intelligences in action is to announce the topic to be studied and get your students to suggest the ways in which it can be approached. This works brilliantly well at all levels as each student finds their own way to be engaged in the task. With the added bonus that they inadvertently stray into, and develop skills in, other intelligences as well.

You can also group students with the same or overlapping intelligences to work on a topic together, or mix and match them into groups of different intelligences, stipulating that everyone has to have an input. This approach can be immense fun. Let's use studying Shakespeare's *Othello* as an example:

- Othello as a bold and fierce lion who speaks in rap (Naturalist and Musical)

- a diary entry of Iago's is discovered explaining why he is so evil (Linguistic and Intrapersonal)

- rearrangement of classroom into a mock-up of Desdemona's bedroom (Spatial and Bodily-Kinaesthetic)

- compile ratio of Iago's evil acts to Othello's gullibility and use as Iago's defence in a mock courtroom (Logical-Mathematical and Interpersonal).

As shown above, you could set each group the challenge of combining two intelligences into the learning. Make the combinations as far-fetched as you like; at this point you want the students to connect with the subject in any way they can. By developing their own 'hook', the students have a better chance of remembering the information and maybe even interesting themselves enough to want to learn more. Don't forget that learning should include an aspect of continual feedback or assessment. How can an individual's assessment reflect their natural intelligences? How can we measure an individual's improvement in an intelligence that is *not* ordinarily natural to them? Again, perhaps the best people to start with are the students themselves and in this way they will start to see and appreciate each other's strengths and watch out for their improvements. Get them to suggest appropriately 'intelligent' ways that their understanding could be measured. Or ideas for how to give feedback to each other.

Take another look at the *Othello* example; how does each of the ideas for representing aspects of *Othello* actually help a student *understand* the play? How can a student be tested to see if the understanding has happened?

Overall, by offering students the concept of multiple intelligences we are encouraging them to accept the idea that individuals can develop in many ways. Or, at the very least we leave the door open for our students to explore it further for themselves one day.

Moving on from Gardner's multiple intelligences, but in a similar vein, I challenge you to start doing regular work-outs with your students. Oh yes, it's time you all took better care of yourselves so no excuses, no waiting for New Year to make a resolution, get on it now. No wait, where are you going? Off to the GYM? Well, that's up to you, but I was referring to a *mental* workout. As you will see in Chapter 4, I can make a bit of a fuss about habits. Habits actually rule our lives and without them our brains just simply wouldn't be able to function as brilliantly as they do. But they can also be counter-productive, especially when we are trying to learn something or be creative. That comfort zone we're so often urged to get out of is in fact the accumulation of all our habits. The *Mental workout* exercise on page 46 plays around a bit with comfort zones and habits and can be a really interesting way to find out more about your students. Oh yes, and they will learn more about you too . . .

This type of activity fits in well with Gardner's multiple intelligences because the whole class will get to see what challenges people choose and how they approach them. People can select challenges that they like the sound of and will find enjoyable and easy, or they choose a challenge to really push themselves into the unknown. If you are brave, you can get the class to choose the challenges you undertake, or at least select from a list you have pre-screened (chicken!). Challenges can be set over a week or term, depending on how often you see your class; we don't want GCSE Chemistry falling by the wayside while you're all engrossed in seeking out new foods or obsessing about that tricky past tense in Hungarian. Choosing a whole-class topic to study is fun too. This is when you all decide to learn about a set topic, go off and do it and come back together to explore all the different ways you went about it. That links in very nicely with the *Research and report game* on page 57 which is an exercise in Chapter 3, Mission Control, but you can use it here as it can work really well as a way of understanding people's different inspiration and strategies for learning.

While we're on the subject of learning together, Ian named a whole raft of organisations and programmes to develop student thinking skills. These types of skills help students understand how they think and, more crucially, how they can then apply these thinking processes to other situations. This exploration of thinking skills stemmed from the work of Reuven Feuerstein, who devised a set of activities to help the cognition of severely disadvantaged children in the 1950s. Since then the study and development of thinking skills has come on in leaps and bounds with general consensus on the main features:

- The focus is on how the learning is happening, i.e. the process.

- Students articulate their thinking/learning so as to make it more visible.

- Students name their learning so it becomes meaningful to them.

- There is collaboration, cooperation and support between students, which teachers are to facilitate.

- Students take responsibility for their own learning.

- Students use a mechanism to make informed decisions.

- Students reflect, monitor and self-evaluate.

- Students are encouraged to transfer their learning into other contexts.

- The classroom is a safe environment to make mistakes.

- The class becomes a community of learning.

In 2003 the NUT produced a really excellent report cataloguing all the thinking skills resources available in the UK. Although now over ten years old, the range of resources and references is amazing and will give anyone interested in learning more about thinking skills a thorough start in the subject. Just search for 'Teaching thinking skills – selected resources 2003' and you can download a ten-page PDF. As ever, see the online resources for this direct link and others.

Brilliant as the concept of teaching thinking skills is, no one is suggesting that this is the model that should be used in every lesson. In fact most advocates recommend running a specific thinking skills session once every fortnight because thinking itself is extremely exhausting. But what we're aiming for here is to repeat the experience often enough so that the understanding becomes embedded and our students will be able to use apt and useful thinking habits whenever the situation arises. Because that's what we're all about here, isn't it? Teaching facts, processes and skills that will be useful in 'the outside world'.

This appears to be an appropriate point at which to remind you actually how unlike the outside world school is. Setting aside for the moment the fact that a student's 'job' at school is to learn lots of things and then be tested on them, the actual *process* required to get through a school day is an immense strain. As I just mentioned, thinking is exhausting. Learning is exhausting. School is exhausting. Though I suspect you may have an inkling about that. An optimum learning situation cannot happen when both you and your students are exhausted. Full-on learning is not effective without pace. You might have the most fantastic, entertaining, informative, interactive, oh-my-golly-gosh-look-at-THAT type of lesson planned, but the truth of the matter is that students may only have the mental energy to retain around 20 per cent of what you are hoping to impart.

Meet my friend Mr Pareto. You may have heard of Pareto's Law or, more possibly, the 80/20 rule. Vilfredo Pareto was a formerly little known and rather grumpy economist and sociologist who, through his obsession with economic synthesis, noticed that wealth distribution in Italy followed a pattern. This led him to the, now famous, observation that 80 per cent of the land in Italy was owned by 20 per cent of the population. Many people had also noticed similar distribution patterns in their own fields of expertise, but it took quality management pioneer Dr Joseph Juran to declare a universal principle he called the 'vital few and trivial many'. Unfortunately Juran accidently made it appear he was attributing his findings to Pareto's work and the name Pareto's Law stuck. There's a lesson in that for us all.

In spite of being called a 'law', it is not. The 80/20 rule is merely an observation that can be interesting when applied to thorny issues such as: do 20 per cent of the students in your school account for 80 per cent of the 'incidents'? Is 80 per cent of the playground taken up with the activities of only 20 per cent of the kids? Do 20 per cent of the staff always take up 80 per cent of talking time at any given meeting? At this stage many people consider they have learned the 80/20 idea and start applying it willy-nilly to any number of situations. Business management being one of them. Imagine being told you have a meeting with your boss to discuss your 20 per cent productivity. What is important to note is that neither Pareto nor Juran meant their observations to be taken so literally and I don't mean that we have to stick rigidly to 80/20; of course there is leeway in the numbers: 99/1, 90/10 and 70/30 are just as commonly found and acceptable as ratios. What I mean is what do we *do* with the numbers?

What is often overlooked, but essential to know, is that Juran later changed his universal principle from the 'vital few and trivial many' to the 'vital few and the *useful* many'. See the difference? This mistake is often made when applying the 80/20 rule, thinking that the 80 per cent doesn't play an important part.

And in the classroom? Well, I have found the 80/20 rule to be amazingly effective. But possibly not in the way you might imagine.

Ian's explanation about the primacy and recency effect fits beautifully into the concept of 80/20 in the classroom. In the way he suggested that memory of what has been learned dips as time progresses and then peaks again before a break, we could extrapolate that the two ends of the session where the memory is best constitute the 20 per cent, and the time spent dipping down and back up again is the 80 per cent. In this case, however, I venture to say the 80 per cent is just as important and can be as useful as the 20 per cent. No, not for learning, but for the ancient art of *mulling*.

Ahhh, mulling and I go back a long way. It was hard at first for me to acknowledge that 'time off' was necessary for things to progress. But I don't think it's any secret to say that spending time away from the learning can produce the insights necessary for that learning to make sense. Sometimes it feels counter-intuitive to step away from something you are finding hard to grasp, but the break and the mull allow your subconscious mind to take over. Your best friend every time. These days I can also call on mulling's close cousin 'busyness' to help me pass the time while I'm waiting for an outcome or insight. Both mulling and busyness are good things to model to your students and should be encouraged in the classroom.

Let's say you have 70 minutes to teach your students two-point perspective:

- 5 minutes **preparation**: Come in and get settled with paper taped in place on boards, equipment at the ready.

- 10 minutes **instruction**: The learning which takes the form of you demonstrating the principles of perspective on the whiteboard or screen and completing a simple drawing of a house and them reproducing each step as you progress. End result is everyone has completed the simple drawing and is pretty chuffed at how 3D their house looks.

- 20 minutes **play**: Time now available for mulling or busyness depending on what each student feels they need to do. Activities might include any or all of these:

  - repeating the same exercise over again from memory, varying the sizes of the houses

  - sketching or doodling the process freehand

  - finding perspective viewpoints inside the classroom and photographing them

  - finding similar perspective images in architectural magazines, sticking them onto paper and finding each vanishing point

  - watching, assisting or helping another student to complete any of the above

- 5 minutes **instruction**: An additional learning session where your students quickly draw up the house again and are then shown how to add windows, doors, architectural features, fences, pavements, gardens, etc. Following on from this, the students can continue to add as many features as they want and can ask anyone else to help them work out the tricky details.

- 15 minutes **play**: A second session of individual activity when students are encouraged to play around with what they have just learned. They are encouraged to make mistakes, see what happens when they break the perspective rules and be ambitious in their drawings.

- 10 minutes *informal* instruction: Bringing it all together to sum up in the last ten minutes. At this point anyone can show what they have done, demonstrate their techniques or ask for a solution to a tricky perspective issue they were struggling with.

- 5 minutes **exit**: Stash the drawings, pack away the drawing boards and exit, buzzing with new learning.

The flow being:

– Preparation – Instruction / Play / Instruction / Play / Instruction – Exit –

At each play point the students choose their activity according to their energy and inclination. Some may want to experiment more, some may want to dream and doodle a bit, some will want an activity they can get up and do, some will want help or will be happy to watch someone else.

The mulling part in this lesson was activity based but it can take many forms in other lessons. Referring back to the range of intelligences, any or all of these types of mulling could be used for starters:

Quietly discussing with your neighbour	Doodling	Practising a physical technique in your mind
Collecting, sorting, organising	Writing thoughts or reflections	Hearing gentle music as you think back over the topic
Walking outside, looking up at the sky	Stretching	Sketching a diagram
Linking learning to interests and ambitions	Repeating the simple learning steps over and over again	Imagining or modelling a key person
Generating a rhythm or chant	Reviewing or listing steps	Canvassing others' opinions about your work

In this type of lesson the learning bit takes 20 per cent of the time and the mulling bit 80 per cent, but what is happening in the mulling part, which also doubles as

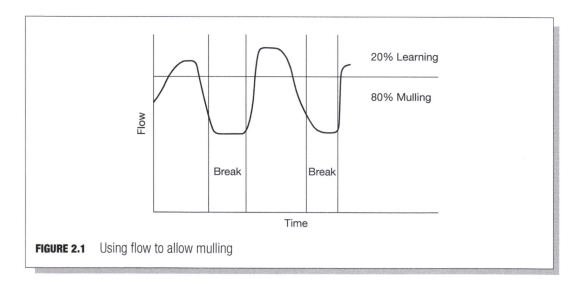

FIGURE 2.1 Using flow to allow mulling

a 'break' from learning, is that the brain assimilates what has just been learned. By allowing students to mull and play with the learning, *in a way that is meaningful to them*, they take ownership of it and are more likely to retain the information. I am sure this idea of only 'teaching' for 20 per cent of the lesson may strike some people as controversial, but what we're playing to here is the natural rhythm of the process of learning and the natural tendencies of your students. So the teaching part is about the *essence* of the subject. The key facts. The nub of the matter. The part that, if omitted, nothing else would make sense. The rest of the learning occurs naturally through each student's own inclinations.

It goes back to the exhausting day that we all experience at school: too much information flying around, too many changes in the day, too much energy required. By reducing each lesson to just its *core* learning, the key message you want your students to retain may just about hang on in there. This is, of course, more necessary for the secondary sector with its chopping and changing between lessons, but there is still a huge amount of learning to be packed into an average primary day and a surprisingly large amount of chopping and changing. And, of course, in the primary classroom you largely have a less sophisticated and self-aware student, which is when the usefulness of Garner's multiple intelligences becomes apparent again.

If you like the 80/20 mulling/learning idea, you might also be a fan of the flipped classroom. This is where the homework part of the learning is taught through video instruction and the school part of the learning centres on discussion of the findings. It's an idea that has been around since 2007 but is gaining traction now and you may well be familiar with its benefits. If you aren't, or if you think it's going to be a trial to set up and run yourself, please grab a cuppa and come with me for a bit of surfing . . .

Of course the wonderful TED-Ed is onto this idea and they have it all sorted for you; just register with them (it's free) and you will get a lovely email explaining how to use their online flipped class resource. Easy peasy and you can get in there to start right away, no prior knowledge needed. You might also like to go online and find a website called the Daily Riff and search for the article 'The Flipped Class: Myths vs Reality'. There are loads of other really interesting articles on that website too. A further great site to search for ideas is Educators Technology, but you may find yourself completely lost and overwhelmed by the sheer number of resources on there (I sure did!) so you can cut straight to the flipped classroom tools by searching for 'best tools and apps'. Flip or don't flip. If you like the idea, these links and more are in the online resources.

As this chapter of self-discovery winds to an end, there could be no one better to sum it all up:

Until you make the unconscious conscious, it will direct your life and you will call it fate.

Carl Jung

Gardner's intelligences quick quiz

Score how true each statement is 0 = Never 1 = Sometimes 2 = Often 3 = Always →		(You don't need this bit until the end)
I like to create my own music		Musical
I like to make up my own experiments		Logical-Mathematical
I like to walk about or move when I'm thinking		Bodily-Kinaesthetic
I like to work in groups		Interpersonal
I am good at spelling		Linguistic
I find charts and diagrams easy to understand		Spatial
I talk to other people about my problems		Interpersonal
I like jigsaw puzzles		Spatial
I can see what a project is going to look like before I start it		Spatial
I like to work by myself		Intrapersonal
I think problems through carefully		Logical-Mathematical
I enjoy being outdoors		Naturalist
I can easily tell if someone likes or dislikes me		Interpersonal
I like to read or listen to stories		Linguistic
I always have a song in my head		Musical
I can run, jump and balance really well		Bodily-Kinaesthetic
I enjoy sorting and organising		Logical-Mathematical
I have a good memory for names, dates and information		Linguistic
I like drawing and art		Spatial
I enjoy word games, puns, tongue-twisters and poetry		Linguistic
I love animals and pets		Naturalist
I learn best by doing things		Bodily-Kinaesthetic
I find some music makes me happy, some makes me cry		Musical
I like writing in a journal or diary		Intrapersonal
I find mental arithmetic (doing sums in my head) easy		Logical-Mathematical
I set goals for myself in the future		Intrapersonal
I enjoy playing sports or dancing		Bodily-Kinaesthetic
I enjoy spending time alone		Intrapersonal
I like to spend time with people rather than alone		Interpersonal

© 2015 *A Teacher's Companion to Essential Motivation in the Classroom*, Georgia Holleran and Ian Gilbert, Routledge

I am interested in the weather		Naturalist
I enjoy growing plants and gardening		Naturalist
I can play a musical instrument		Musical

Add the totals for each intelligence type and put them in the boxes below: ⟶

Linguistic	
Logical-Mathematical	
Musical	
Bodily-Kinaesthetic	
Spatial	
Interpersonal	
Intrapersonal	
Naturalist	

My top-scoring intelligences are:

1.

2.

3.

Gardner's multiple intelligences descriptors

Linguistic				
Can include all or some of these:				
Loves to read	Loves to write stories or poetry	Likes debating	Enjoys talking about ideas	Keeps a diary or journal
Enjoys learning other languages	Has a wide vocabulary	Enjoys listening to stories	Can spell well	Likes writing emails or letters
Likes puns and tongue-twisters	Likes to tell stories	Enjoys word games	Has a good memory for facts	Enjoys researching

How to use linguistic intelligence to improve the others:

Linguistic – get *even better*: join a book club, write to a favourite author, learn another language	Logical-Mathematical: silently talk through maths problems, catalogue personal reading books
Musical: write songs or lyrics, find out more about a composer or songwriter	Bodily-Kinaesthetic: take part in plays or productions, draw huge letterforms in the air
Spatial: take time to imagine the scenes or characters in stories, describe a famous painting	Interpersonal: carefully listen to others when they talk, read about body language
Intrapersonal: keep a diary or journal, write out personal problems to understand them better	Naturalist: read about myths in other cultures, research the natural world around you

Brilliant careers:

Lawyer	Counsellor	Public speaker	Playwright	Sales person
Commentator	Novelist	Poet	Journalist	Politician
Translator	Magazine editor	Librarian	TV presenter	Storyteller
Copywriter	Screenwriter	Teacher	Author	Indexer

Logical-Mathematical				
Can include all or some of these:				
Enjoys counting and cataloguing	Likes working on the computer	Is very neat and tidy	Can do mental maths easily	Enjoys making charts and graphs
Makes up experiments	Connects actions to outcomes	Fascinated by numbers	Remembers scores and statistics	Is good at guessing or estimating
Likes chess or draughts	Makes up secret codes	Enjoys brainteasers and logic puzzles	Enjoys solving mysteries	Enjoys science

How to use logical-mathematical intelligence to improve the others:

Linguistic: read mysteries, read about science, write about favourite topics	Logical-Mathematical – get *even better*: watch science programmes, practise mental maths
Musical: listen for musical patterns, learn to read music, use music creation software	Bodily-Kinaesthetic: notice statistics in sports, see how people calculate angles and distances

Spatial: look for patterns in science, experiment with computer animation		Interpersonal: play chess, draughts, card or board games, notice people's strategies,	
Intrapersonal: make a website about something you are interested in, write a list of your future goals		Naturalist: research interesting processes like photosynthesis, erosion and weather systems	

Brilliant careers:				
Astronaut	Inventor	Programmer	Bookkeeper	Scientist
Statistician	Accountant	Researcher	Game designer	Broker
Engineer	Webmaster	Negotiator	Quality surveyor	Treasurer
Analyst	Technical writer	Banker	Detective	Auditor

Musical
Can include all or some of these:

Writes own songs	Enjoys making musical sounds	Enjoys singing	Can rap	Can read music
Often has a song in their head	Can sing a tune straight back	Remembers facts by using songs	Plays an instrument	Likes listening to music
Recognises tunes very quickly	Sings or hums when busy	Can read music	Likes different styles of music	Easily picks up rhythms

How to use musical intelligence to improve the others:	
Linguistic: learn spellings to music or rhymes, hear the sounds in stories	Logical-Mathematical: learn lists and formulas to music, notice the logical construction of sheet music
Musical – get *even better*: listen to a wide range of music, watch live bands and orchestras	Bodily-Kinaesthetic: move to music, tap your toes, nod your head, dance, clap
Spatial: see the pictures that music creates in your mind, create a collage based on music	Interpersonal: make music with others, see how they enjoy music, listen to how they talk about it
Intrapersonal: notice the emotions music makes you feel and think about why	Naturalist: notice tunes and melodies in nature, notice also the city noises and sounds

Brilliant careers:				
Instrument maker	Voice coach	Musician	Conductor	Sound engineer
Music journalist	Foley artist	Instrument tuner	Singer	Jingle writer
Studio director	Acoustic engineer	Composer	DJ	Music producer
Entertainer	Songwriter	Music teacher	Music therapist	Video designer

Bodily-Kinaesthetic
Can include all or some of these:

Likes movement and activity	Can mimic people's expressions	Loves practical lessons	Is skilful at building models	Dances gracefully and rhythmically
Learns physical skills easily	Thinks better when moving around	Has a good sense of co-ordination	Can climb and balance well	Enjoys exploring new places

Plays sports well	Enjoys learning in different places	Enjoys making things	Likes role-play and acting	Has a good sense of timing

How to use bodily-kinaesthetic intelligence to improve the others:	
Linguistic: spell using movable magnetic letters, write spellings large in the air	Logical-Mathematical: design and build something, practise estimating and measuring sports progress
Musical: notice the rhythms and patterns when dancing, exercise to music with different beats	Bodily-Kinaesthetic – get *even better*: learn a sport, dance or crafts skill, learn how to keep fit
Spatial: use modelling materials, experiment with ways to make marks, explore buildings	Interpersonal: learn magic tricks and how to keep or distract people's attention
Intrapersonal: create thinking time by running, yoga, tai chi and swimming	Naturalist: notice signs of nature when out, feel the wind, the warmth or the rain

Brilliant careers:				
Magician	Actor	Hairdresser	Lifeguard	Choreographer
Soldier	Dentist	Dancer	Driver	Crafts maker
Builder	Coach	Chef	Stunt person	Surgeon
Diver	Fire-fighter	Explorer	Athlete	Circus performer

Spatial
Can include all or some of these:

Likes puzzles and optical illusions	Likes building 3D models	Can see objects clearly in mind	Loves using arts and crafts	Likes doodling and drawing
Easily reads maps and diagrams	Enjoys films and videos	Thinks in pictures	Learns by watching others	Sees patterns in everything
Likes to problem solve by drawing	Notices shapes and styles	Has a great visual memory	Plays lots of video games	Makes diagrams to help learning

How to use spatial intelligence to improve the others:	
Linguistic: see how poetry and illustrations work together, make a comic book	Logical-Mathematical: use diagrams to think through problems, notice mathematical patterns
Musical: notice the pictures that music makes, use music for inspiration	Bodily-Kinaesthetic: use different parts of the body to create art or sculpture, physically move about
Spatial – get *even better*: learn more about great artists and designers, make videos	Interpersonal: teach others how to be creative, play visual games with other people
Intrapersonal: make a vision board for the future, design ideal clothes or environments	Naturalist: try orienteering, photograph the natural world, draw maps of the area

Brilliant careers:				
Surveyor	Photographer	Graphic designer	Artist	Cartographer
Interior designer	Illustrator	Film director	Inventor	Product developer

Window dresser	Decorator	Cartoonist	Fashion designer	Civil engineer
Pilot	Sculptor	Web designer	Animator	Crafts maker

Interpersonal Can include all or some of these:				
Likes to work with others	Watches others	Aware of fairness	Likes group activities	Can be persuasive
Happy to meet new people	Can tell how someone is feeling	Makes friends easily	Likes to organise activities	Is a good listener
Can interview others well	Offers to help others	Likes lively conversations	Can enthuse others	Knows how to help people get along

How to use interpersonal intelligence to improve the others:	
Linguistic: talk about books, practise spellings with others, write and direct a play	Logical-Mathematical: start a maths or science study group, write and run quizzes
Musical: ask people what music they like and why, join a local musical theatre or choral group	Bodily-Kinaesthetic: learn social activities like martial arts or dancing, join a sports team
Spatial: join or run an arts and crafts club, design and make a community mural	Interpersonal – get *even better*: volunteer to help others, get a mentor, learn to be a leader
Intrapersonal: list existing social skills and set goals for improving or adding to them	Naturalist: join an environmental cause, talk to people about their love of the natural world

Brilliant careers:				
Actor	Politician	Sociologist	Psychiatrist	Talk show host
Police officer	Therapist	Health professional	Coach	Salesperson
Manager	Personal assistant	Teacher	Consultant	Mentor
Psychologist	Social worker	Business owner	Travel agent	Criminologist

Intrapersonal Can include all or some of these:				
Knows own strengths	Loves keeping a journal or diary	Prefers to work alone	Self-assured	Happy in own company
Looks after themselves	Likes setting personal goals	Stands up for own opinions	Can work through own problems	Knows own shortcomings
Aware of own feelings	Has a great imagination	Dreams about the future	Likes to write about thoughts	Can resist peer pressure

How to use intrapersonal intelligence to improve the others:	
Linguistic: write an autobiography, keep a journal to put ideas and thoughts in	Logical-Mathematical: learn how the mind works, make connections between favourite activities
Musical: learn to play a favourite song, pay attention to the emotions music stirs up	Bodily-Kinaesthetic: use dance, mime or acting to express feelings, learn focus through meditation

| Spatial: create a self-portrait, use different arts to express feelings, visit different environments | | Interpersonal: find people with similar interests, notice how people deal with different situations | | |
| Intrapersonal – get *even better*: make a list of ways to deal with problems, set targets and goals | | Naturalist: notice feelings associated with being outside in nature, collect pictures and reminders | | |

Brilliant careers:				
Detective	Inventor	Actor	Biographer	Writer
Comedian	Artist	Psychologist	Counsellor	Film director
Philosopher	Researcher	Entrepreneur	Teacher	Psychiatrist
Personal trainer	Therapist	Performance artist	Lifestyle coach	Theorist

Naturalist Can include all or some of these:				
Always notices nature	Enjoys growing plants	Loves animals	Enjoys finding out about animals	Is street smart
Likes visiting parks and zoos	Might be a vegetarian	Keen to learn about nature	Cares about the environment	Loves camping
Prefers learning outdoors	Remembers plant names	Can adapt well to surroundings	Can talk about the weather	Has outdoor related hobbies

How to use naturalist intelligence to improve the others:				
Linguistic: read more about interests, make notes about findings, talk to others about interests		Logical-Mathematical: invent science experiments, classify and categorise interests		
Musical: listen for natural music when outside, make music with natural materials		Bodily-Kinaesthetic: notice how nature affects all the senses, hike, walk or run in the fresh air		
Spatial: capture nature in photos or artworks, spot patterns and textures, visit large spaces		Interpersonal: start a community garden, teach others about nature, talk to naturalists		
Intrapersonal: notice emotions and feelings when in nature, research jobs linked with interests		Naturalist – get *even better*: take care of a plant or pet, create an ecosystem, study astronomy		

Brilliant careers:				
Animal trainer	Photographer	Conservationist	Archaeologist	Gardener
Vet	Landscaper	Farmer	Pet therapist	Zoologist
Biologist	Meteorologist	Nursery owner	Fisher	Beekeeper
Gamekeeper	Zoo keeper	Tree surgeon	Herbalist	Palaeontologist

Who's who

Which person demonstrates which intelligence? Hint: they may have more than one . . .

Linguistic	Logical-Mathematical	Musical	Bodily-Kinaesthetic

Spatial	Interpersonal	Intrapersonal	Naturalist

Maya Angelou	Albert Einstein	William Shakespeare	Dame Kelly Holmes	Hillary Clinton
Salvador Dali	Marie Curie	Oprah Winfrey	Aristotle	Tony Robbins
Mother Theresa	Tiger Woods	Pablo Picasso	Pavarotti	Taylor Swift
Barack Obama	Paul McKenna	Michael Jackson	Margaret Thatcher	Eminem
Anne Frank	Stephen Hawking	Isambard Kingdom Brunel	Mahatma Gandhi	David Beckham
Steve Irwin	Thomas Edison	Charles Darwin	J.K. Rowling	Pink
Beethoven	Simon Cowell	Friedrich Nietzsche	Joy Adamson	Ted Hughes
Michael Jordan	Barbara Hepworth	Mozart	Norman Foster	Fearne Cotton
Tony Hawk	Georgia O'Keeffe	Bill Gates	Fred Astaire	Capability Brown

Brilliant intelligences activities list

Brilliant things for
Linguistic thinkers

Reading stories	Learning a new language	Discussions	Poems
Debates	Rapping	Synonyms and antonyms	Rhyming words
Speeches	Listening games	Explaining	Writing a diary or journal
Learning a new word each week	Designing a slogan	Making a radio advert	Upwords
Writing an article	Designing marketing posters	Writing letters	Creating a magazine
Crosswords	Writing a project	Reading newspapers	Cockney rhyming slang
Presentations	Boggle	*Call My Bluff* panel game	Reading aloud
Tongue-twisters	Listening to radio plays	Scrabble	Starting a blog
Hangman	Write reviews	Codeword puzzles	Designing anagrams

Brilliant things for
Logical-Mathematical thinkers

Creating graphs	Hnefatafl	Calculating percentages	Solving mysteries
Battleships	Recording measurements	Making charts	*Mastermind* board game
Showing explanations in a diagram	Solving puzzles	Forecasts	Estimation games
Riddles	Playing with numbers	Analysis and explanation	Mental maths
Making patterns	Statistics	Organising and cataloguing	Strategy games
Budgeting	Measuring cause and effect	Chess	Tracking progress
Draughts	Guessing games	Designing experiments	Following recipes and instructions
Computer gaming	Counting and recording	Creating accounts	Cluedo
Extrapolating conclusions	Calculating ratios	Predicting outcomes	Organising sequences
Tidying and organising belongings	Lateral thinking	Designing secret codes	Plotting co-ordinates

Brilliant things for
Musical thinkers

Mystery sounds game	Writing songs and tunes	Background music	Visualisation to music
Rapping	Nursery rhymes with new words	Beatboxing	Making up jingles
Historical music	Using the body to make musical sounds	Composing lyrics	Rhyming
Name that tune	Alliteration	Rhythms	Classroom entrance and exit music
Music with learning messages	Ditties	Natural sounds and birdsong	Football chants
Songs as memory aids	Intros game	Mozart or Beethoven in class	Cultural or geographical music

Brilliant things for
Bodily-Kinaesthetic thinkers

Field trips	Physical cutting and pasting	Role-play	Gut feelings and intuition
Cookery	Constructing models	Making physical effort to achieve something	Handling artefacts
Drama and re-enactment	Balancing	Making videos	Routines
Construction puzzles	Weighing up and estimating	Large size jigsaws	Lego
Acting	Meditation and relaxation	Making crafts	Walking through the learning
Mending and fixing	Jenga	Dancing and movement	Practical exercises
3D printing	Cranium	Warming up and cooling down	Modelling clay
Juggling	Excavating	Twister	Testing reflexes and stamina
Catching and throwing	Competitive games	Magic tricks	Charades
Metal puzzles	Rubik's cube	Mapping the surroundings	Mime

Brilliant things for Spatial thinkers

Symbols and icons	Constructing models	Photography	Inventing and designing
A visual journal	Diagrams	Arts and craft activities	Textures
Puzzles	Charts and graphs	Visualising	Finding and constructing patterns
Taking things apart and reassembling	Tangrams	Creative challenges	Highlighter pens
Mapping the learning	Computer animation	Optical illusions	Organising space
Daydreaming	Visual instructions	Dingbats	Instructive display work
Making and watching videos	Flick books	Bullet points	Jigsaws
Posters	Meccano	Observation	Playing online games and puzzles
Imagining	Sketching ideas out first	Brainstorming	Origami
Kaleidoscopes	Cartooning and caricaturing	Pairs	Rush hour game
Pictionary	Colour and shape	Historical arts and design	Technical drawing

Brilliant things for Interpersonal thinkers

Active listening	Volunteering	Group work	Monitoring for fairness
Observing others	Interviewing	Resolving conflicts	Leading a team
Co-ordinating an activity	Using intuition	*Family Fortunes*	Lively discussions
Would I lie to you?	Body language	Teaching others	Mediating and negotiating
Forming a club	Competitive team games	Smiling	Modelling success
Chat shows	Assisting others	Debating and persuading	*Golden Balls*
Fronting a cause or campaign	Developing networks	Sharing thoughts and ideas	Organising a celebration
Standing for school council	Solving people's problems	Mentoring	Public speaking

Brilliant things for Intrapersonal thinkers

Setting goals and targets	WIIFMs	Journaling	Using memories and artefacts
Thinking about thinking	Daydreaming	Planning own study	Modelling others
Expressing feelings	Making mistakes	Emotional intelligence	Understanding emotions
Imagining	Justifying own ideas	Judging outcomes of events	Working on own projects
Finding a mentor	Understanding own feelings	Reflective thinking	Philosophy
Empathy	Independent thought	Personality quizzes	Speculating on the future
Identifying personal improvement	Questioning	Using tools to aid thinking	Spiritual thinking
Autobiographies and biographies	Talking to others	Careers	Make own self-help manual

Brilliant things for Naturalist thinkers

Identifying and classifying	Patterns and shapes in nature	Field trips and visits	Observing
Tracking	Exploration	Being out of the classroom	Caring for animals and plants
Predicting weather	Environmental causes	Questioning and interviewing	Keeping a nature journal
Handling and touching	Giving characters animal traits	Physical geography	Excavating
Gaining energy by gazing at the sky	Repairing and fixing	Making herbal remedies	Floral and natural smells
Being barefoot	Growing and cooking fruit and vegetables	Healing	Outdoor construction

Mental workout

Challenge your students to do something new once a week and tell you and the rest of the class about it. There are many ways this can be done:

1. Read from a newspaper you wouldn't usually read
2. Watch a TV programme you wouldn't ordinarily watch
3. Find a TED talk that wouldn't usually interest you
4. Try a new food
5. Research a job or career that you wouldn't normally be interested in
6. Visit a place you've never been to
7. Start a conversation with someone in school you don't know very well
8. Choose a very different book to read from the library
9. Cook something you've never cooked before
10. Try a craft you've never tried
11. Learn about superfoods and introduce them into your meals, one a week
12. Interview someone interesting about their life
13. Learn a new skill on a computer
14. Learn a magic trick a week
15. Learn a different sign in sign language every week
16. Learn a new word in a different language every week
17. Learn a new word in English every week!
18. Find a destination in the world and research how you would get there
19. Start an exercise routine, one exercise per week
20. Learn to juggle
21. Volunteer for something
22. Teach something to someone else
23. Talk to an elderly person about what their school days were like
24. Watch a documentary about something you wouldn't usually be interested in
25. Plant something in a window box or garden
26. Try karaoke
27. Write with your non-dominant hand (not in class and not whilst signing anything!)
28. Take a different route to school or another regular destination
29. Notice, or get someone to tell you, a habit of yours, then break it
30. Produce a self-portrait
31. Learn to identify ten common trees in the UK
32. Make an item of clothing to wear
33. Write a letter or email to someone famous asking them a question
34. Visit an exhibition, gallery or museum that you wouldn't normally
35. Learn the lyrics of a song
36. Watch a local team play football, cricket or bowls!
37. Organise a sponsored 'something' for charity
38. Wear something you wouldn't normally (don't try this with the school uniform!)
39. Listen to Radio 4 for an hour every day for a week
40. Address an audience about a topic that is in the news this week

And of course you, as the teacher, must set a good example so must also do something new every week and report back . . .

Mission control

Covering these topics:

Allowing students more control
Taking responsibility
Developing multiple approaches to learning
Using physical activities to anchor learning

It takes a very particular sort of 'smart' to go through the school system and come out with no qualifications whatsoever.

Ian Gilbert, *Essential Motivation in the Classroom*

Here we have the crux of many a teacher's issue with the day-to-day job of teaching. Control.

Have you ever watched somebody effortlessly glide through a lesson with every student fully engaged on task and apparently enjoying the whole experience? Ofsted have. And, having been in a number of schools during Ofsted inspections, I can confidently report the teaching and learning during that time is amazing. Schools always get stressed about student behaviour during an inspection and, more often than not, very little really happens. I was once drafted into a school during inspection week to be on hand to 'fight fires as and when needed' and held my breath in anticipation. As it turned out, I wasn't called upon once and at the time I wondered what had happened to the usually quite challenging students. Some years later, and having witnessed what I can only describe as 'Ofsted-induced school harmony' break out in the wildest of terrains, I began to get it: during inspections I noticed two very different and abnormal occurrences. The first being that the students are *choosing* to behave.

Of course they are. Apart from a few hard cases, most students know *exactly* what's required of them in school. They are also very aware of undertones, which leads me to my observation that 'The severity of punishment for misbehaviour increases in direct proportion to how inconveniencing the misbehaviour was at the time.' In other words, most kids *know* not to mess about when Ofsted inspectors are around as the consequences could be proportionally dire. So the assumption is that the rest of the time, though most of your students know how to behave, some are simply choosing not to.

The second reason the Ofsted factor seemed to work was that students were somehow more engaged in their lessons when the inspectors were in. Could it be that lessons are just a tiny bit more planned and prepared when the inspectors are hovering? Yes, of course, everyone makes an effort to show the best side of their classes at these times, but surely it is unrealistic to expect teachers to go to such great lengths as to prepare for every lesson as if it was being watched by Ofsted? Oh yes. Unrealistic and unnecessary.

If you're wanting wonderfully engaged and co-operative students in your classes, then don't over-think, over-plan or over-prepare. Listen to the one thing your students are asking of you. As Ian so beautifully puts it:

> Could it possibly be that there are children misbehaving in our classrooms because they want their happiness back?'
>
> Ian Gilbert, *Essential Motivation in the Classroom*

This comment was prompted by Mihaly Csikszentmihalyi's observations in his must-read book *Flow* that we are motivated by the need to have the flow experience not available in ordinary life. By that he is suggesting that ordinary life does not always provide opportunities for flow. Well no, ordinary life doesn't, but your classroom could! You could have a classroom where your students are experiencing flow every time they set foot inside; even better, if flow is not necessarily forthcoming at any given time, they have enough faith in you and your lessons not to use the opportunity for troublemaking. Bliss?

It's all doable.

Let's give your students their happiness back. Even better, let's teach them how to maintain their own happiness while engaging in the learning you have ready for them. Are you up for it? Can you do whatever it takes? Can you handle the fact that the hideous secret to transforming your classroom into a culture of organically learning minds is to leap into the void and give your students some *responsibility for their own learning*?

Proper responsibility, sustained and supported throughout the school, is a wonderful thing and is happening all over the world in places such as Sudbury Valley School in Massachusetts; Northern Beaches Christian School in New South Wales; Riverside in Gujarat, India; the Lumia Schools in Brazil and the Quest Schools run by the Institute of Play in New York. And you don't need to start from scratch; see the online resources for what happened when Forest Avenue Elementary School in Rhode Island decided to reconfigure what they already had. Could you, with a bit of faith, preparation and co-operation, bring this kind of enthusiasm for learning into your school?

Maybe you can't wait long enough to redesign your entire curriculum or bash down some walls. So what can you do right now? Quite a lot, but before we start to edge our students towards assuming some responsibility for their own happiness, we need to ensure that they consider the classroom a safe place in which to do so. Once you establish some ground rules, you can start to 'brand' your lessons in such a way that your students will learn to relax and let go of the need to be on their guard in case they are going to be asked to do something they can't. There's more about that in Chapter 6, but a simple start could be to get the students to construct some class rules. Many primary classrooms spell out their rules for co-operative behaviour, but these don't seem to be found as frequently on the walls in secondary schools. I like simple rules that apply to the teacher just as much as the student:

- smile

- be clear about the learning

- no blame / no failure / constructive criticism only

48

- use each other's strengths and interests – students as mini-teachers

- be aware of the energy flow.

The *Class rules* exercise on page 55 can help you get the students' perspective, and once you have a suitable collection of ideas for rules, you can display them any way you like:

- Have them running around the top of the walls like a stock-market ticker display.

- Have them pop up in unusual places: on the ceiling, inside cupboard doors, inside roller blinds. The element of surprise causes them not to become part of the scenery and ignored.

- Go mad and have them printed onto a T-shirt. Don't feel obliged to wear the T-shirt, unless you're that kind of wacky teacher; there will always be someone else in the class who'll oblige. And when the students get older and too cool to wear it, bring in a mascot or shop dummy. As I am aware that my inclinations will always tend towards the theatrical, I'll stop short at suggesting you make flags or bunting . . .

- Print the rules out so they can be stuck on the front cover of student books or folders where they can see them. Students can obviously design their own, but not so decoratively that they cannot be read.

The idea is to make the students aware of how your classroom operates and remind them of the expected behaviour. Mentioning key rules in introductions and during explanations helps reinforce them: 'OK people, if each group would tell us their conclusions now, safe in the knowledge we're in a constructive criticism *only* environment.' (Winning smile.)

It's worth noting that, as in the film *Fight Club*, short rules tend to be easier to remember. And, while you're at it, why not invest in a few key posters? There's a number from this book ready to download from the online resources and each poster is also shown on pages 125–144. I am quite fond of Ian's observation that people can be classified as either DDMs or DMDs. 'Don't Do, Moan' or 'Don't Moan, Do'. Which one are you? Can you identify these characteristics in your students? Your colleagues? Sneak that poster into the staffroom, I dare you.

Once the ground rules have been established, it is time to start handing over the leash of responsibility and loosening your control. Beware though, this could get messy. Exploration is messy. Grasping understanding is messy.

Learning.

Is.

Messy.

If you are one of those neat and orderly types, it's probably best to look away now.

I once collected a class together and tossed a solitary envelope onto the table in front of them. In the envelope was their mission: they had six weeks to get organised before going up in front of four dragons from local industry to pitch their money-making ideas. They sat there for a bit, then asked me what to do next. I said it was all up to them. Then they sat there a bit more. When they gradually got the idea that they were pretty much on their own when it came to lesson content, a few interesting developments happened. One of the 'liveliest' characters declared that the class would have to organise themselves so started an election process to determine a class leader.

That done, the elected leader decided to split the class into groups to brainstorm ideas and then to present the best ideas to the rest of the class for comments as to which should be developed. The groups were self-formed so mainly consisted of friends, but interestingly, as the weeks wore on, some students moved to other groups so that they could 'get on better' away from their friends. I'm not saying the whole project flowed by without incident (an occasional quiet chat in the corridor and a few directional steers from myself), but six weeks later they all made their presentations in front of the assembled dragons and actually did themselves proud. And, as a result, they were simply buzzing for days. One or two of their money-making ideas were quite inspired too, including a decorate-your-own-cakes bakery and a cleanable graffiti wall so people could be photographed in front of their own artwork (you saw it here first folks). Perhaps I should mention too that the group consisted of a collection of low-achieving Year 9 students, placed together as an 'art' class because there was really nothing else for them to do . . .

This class was a great illustration of learning in action, but also of something else. They were in a mid-table east London secondary school which exhibited some very obvious poverty within its cohort. As the weeks passed, I learned more about my little group; quite a few were on and off report, literacy was no one's strong point, one student actually never spoke. At all. At first I struggled with the unfairness that these kids were experiencing. But then I was reminded of what I consider to be the most memorable paragraph in Ian's book, which made me see it differently:

> The more I considered the nature of success the more I realised that this sense of responsibility was at the heart of personal achievement. What's more, I began to realise that in many ways a stable home and success in the education system could actually deny an individual the opportunity to take up the challenge of responsibility, that success at school could actually prevent me from achieving my potential beyond school.
>
> Ian Gilbert, *Essential Motivation in the Classroom*

So these students already knew all about challenges; what they didn't know too much about was what they could do to manage challenges. Could these students potentially have some sort of an *advantage* over their seemingly better placed peers born into the middle classes? Remember my daughter learning to ride her bike as a high challenge/low stress activity? School is the perfect place for these students to learn, practise and apply skills for managing challenges, which could help them with the management of the challenges they face in their lives away from school.

Through school students can trial and experiment with the many ways to:

- choose their own interests to research

- construct their own independent work

- present, discuss and defend their opinions

- stretch their creative thinking

- develop their ideas

- manage themselves

- manage being part of a group

- accept responsibility and accountability.

Which all translate beautifully into being a fully operational member of society.

Though the Dragons' Den approach might be too large a leap for your students, you can introduce the experience of taking responsibility for their own learning in much smaller steps. There's certainly mileage to be had with Ian's tried and tested ways to start giving control:

- letting the class choose task A or task B to answer first.

- individuals to choose in which order they tackle the first five questions

- whether the class wants to do their timed essay at the beginning of the lesson or at the end

- whether the class wants their test before or after break.

Another way to allow students to learn in their own way is to consider bringing more choice into the way they access what you are teaching them. Some great ideas to start off your thinking can be found in *Ways to get the students to generate their own learning* on page 56 or *But that's boring!* on page 89.

Ian uses a good example where you write the topic to be studied on the board and then let the students take it from there and find their own ways to seek out the information. A development of this approach is the *Research and report game* on page 57, which can be huge fun if you see a class once a week or you are able to set it as an over-the-weekend challenge. The game centres around a regular feedback session when everyone has to find out an interesting fact about a set topic. The trick is to try to find a fact that no one else will use, which encourages students to be creative and cultivate wide research. You score one point for finding your fact and get two points if no one else uses it. If one of your students is a stats fanatic, they could keep a running score each week. Tips and starter sources of information can be supplied that anyone can access via the LRC (or you might still have a library!) or the internet. A simple research strategy could be to start with a broad scan to check general facts, before narrowing to find a specific aspect to focus on. Tips on how to encourage creative thinking can also be given. For example, students could:

- draw up a thinking map about the topic to help them to consider a range of angles

- use word games to think of unusual combinations; e.g. if the topic is ox bow lake formation, try making connections using a random word generator (check the online resources for the one I used). I tried this just now and the first three words were 'practical', 'lobe' and 'duckweed'. Get that grey matter working!

- find an expert on the topic, either in a book or online, or even drop them an email. Ask them what they love about the topic. Would they do a guest Skype?

- see if there are any useful videos online. TED is usually worth checking, especially TED-Ed

- track down an online forum or discussion group talking about this topic

- link the topic with other school subjects, e.g. ox bow lakes seen through the eyes of Art or Maths or Languages, etc.

Make sure that all evidence and sources of facts are retained so students can show where they obtained their knowledge in case someone challenges the fact as incorrect, or says they are made up! This activity also links brilliantly with marketing your subject, as students generate their own lines of interest connected with your subject. It could also be a useful aside to mention that Wikipedia is created in a similar way. That is to say by a collective of people (though no doubt there is some sort of point scoring going on somewhere).

Other ways to challenge your classes could include looking for inspiration from classic challenge situations and incorporating them into your class activities. How could you incorporate these TV game shows into your topics?

The Krypton Factor	Mastermind	Fifteen to One	Million Pound Drop
Jeopardy	Would I Lie to You?	Call My Bluff	The Crystal Maze
The Weakest Link	Runaround	University Challenge	The Cube
Who Wants to Be a Millionaire?	Countdown	What's My Line?	Blockbusters
Golden Balls	Name That Tune	Treasure Hunt	Scrapheap Challenge

And here's an example of a similar line of inspiration to teach Impressionism through retro pastimes:

- a trivial pursuit game around the lives and works of the impressionists

- each student has a jigsaw piece with part of the Impressionist timeline on it and has to assemble the whole as a team activity

- pairs game matching the artist with the painting

- students to choose an artist from the impressionist period and others to guess identity through the yes/no game

- several impressionist paintings are made into large jigsaws, then all the pieces jumbled; students to identify differences between each style to help them sort and complete them

- individual artist's statistics classified into 'Top Trumps' cards.

And don't for one minute think you have to be the one making all the resources. Why deny your students all the fun? In fact, shouldn't that be what your classes are all about? Fun? Wouldn't it be great if they saw your lessons as play and yet they were still learning by the bucketful?

Told you this could get messy. It's time to introduce more play in your classroom. Play works because students can experience more freedom while engaged in a high challenge/low stress activity potentially inducing flow. It also appeals to those students who benefit from a more active approach to learning, the ones who find thinking while sitting still for long periods of time really hard. There are some brilliant books and websites detailing games and play in the classroom and some will appeal to you more than others. Remember you are operating from your own preferences for learning (more about that in a minute) so you may surprise yourself, and delight your class, if you step outside your ~~comfort~~ habit zone and do something a bit different. Even your vocabulary can make a difference: use phrases like 'just play with that idea for a moment' or 'let's have a quick game using synonyms'.

Another reason using play is so successful in the classroom is because it allows students to be more 'them'. Unfortunately the opportunity to play becomes less and less common in the classroom as students progress through school, and those who don't really feel like themselves when sitting still and listening to the teacher can really start to suffer. If we glance back to Gardner for a moment and consider the intelligences of a child who might be tempted to misbehave in a lesson, it may well be that they have a need for more physical activities or require more frequent new stimulation or challenge. In the 1990s and 2000s the concept of learning styles referred to as VAK (Visual, Auditory and Kinaesthetic, or VARK to include 'reading/writing') was a popular movement in education. This meant that teachers were assessing their students and differentiating their lessons according to each of the three learning styles. Nothing wrong with that as such; in fact many of the 'K' children who preferred to learn by doing probably benefited from the increase in these types of activities, but the identification of being either a V, A or K was way too limiting. The implication was that each person only has one learning style and that it was the one they should do their 'learning' with while ignoring the potential of the others. The British scientist Baroness Greenfield puts the argument against using individual VAK labels rather well:

> Humans have evolved to build a picture of the world through our senses working in unison, exploiting the immense interconnectivity that exists in the brain.

Which is why I keep stressing that ALL assessments are merely a *snapshot of that individual's preferences about that subject, at that time.* But I feel we should not dismiss the whole VAK experience as 'nonsense' (also declared by Baroness Greenfield). Basing an entire curriculum on it might be a bit limiting, but the whole notion of learning through different means certainly isn't. Clearly I am a fan of Gardner's multiple intelligences, but mainly as a starting point to help students understand their natural strengths (perhaps even demonstrate to them for the first time that they *have* strengths). My approach is first to understand what excites the student, then hook that excitement to whatever they are required to understand. The multiple intelligences idea becomes another useful tool for me to understand a bit about them. As do exercises like the *The wish list* (p. 16) and *What makes you happy?* (p. 17) which can both unearth useful insights. So don't dismiss VAK entirely. Know your stuff and blend it wisely.

While we're on the subject of knowing your stuff; do you know what kind of teacher you are? And, more importantly, how your bias (mis)informs you about the content of your lessons? This is what I learned about my own approach to lesson planning:

I like to teach by . . .	It doesn't suit people who . . .
. . . chopping and changing activities	. . . like to drill deeply into a subject
. . . using diagrammatical worksheets and posters	. . . prefer hearing or doing
. . . demonstrating 'the best way'	. . . love to experiment
. . . watching the understanding occur	. . . have to, or like to, mull
. . . providing a 'complete' experience	. . . need to make sense of each part themselves

It was a type of analysis like this that helped me see where I was excluding people who needed different inputs and atmospheres in the classroom. *So much* in teaching is dependent on *who* and *how* you are, I cannot stress enough that to be as effective as possible you need to have an understanding of yourself as much as, if not more than, an understanding of your students. Completing an exercise like the one I did above may help you identify easily filled gaps. If you enjoy a comparison, then consider the lesson I outlined in Chapter 2 on page 31 and how the play activities might have been very different if I had not taken into consideration how my teaching style was excluding some students. If you realise you are excluding certain types of learner, you can include activities to help engage them.

There's a starter list below and, oh wow, don't some of them look like play . . .

Posters	Use colour and highlighters	Balance	Rhymes, chants, songs	Make videos
Ask a friend	Walk through the learning	Map of the learning/ topic	Stand up to think	Visualisation
Teach someone else	Interactive whiteboard	Debates and discussions	Record learning to replay later	Post-it notes
Mime/act out	Active reading	Doodle	Role-play / professional theatre group	Write in the air

It seems like an apt time to reintroduce wonderful Mr Dobbins, as first mentioned by Ian, and the phrase that could start off any learning session with glowingly positive intentions:

You are responsible for your own success, you will go far and I will have achieved a great deal today.

What you might have to bear in mind here is the individual maturity of your students. Schools and classrooms often rely on big assumptions to function with any efficiency at all. The main assumption we have to make is that our students are ready and able to learn when we are ready to teach. It's not a wrong assumption, just not a very realistic model of how we, as humans, work. Imagine saying to a new born baby, 'Right come on now, I've got the weekend free, let's get you walking.' You might be ready, but my bet would be that the baby just hasn't got the capability yet, no matter what tactics you use. But guess what? That baby, given the right encouragement and time to develop, will probably start to take its first steps within the year and, before too long, will be off running down the street with you in hot pursuit in no time. Bearing in mind the human brain fully matures some time between ages 25 and 30, you could be waiting a while for some of your students to be ready. So the thought to ponder on is: are your students misbehaving because they don't want to learn what you're teaching, or are they not ready? Whatever the outcome of your pondering, the conclusion has to be to ensure your classroom is the best environment for encouraging your students to give the best they've got.

And, when it comes to responsibility for learning, you have to take Mr Dobbins' words to heart too. You are not responsible for your students' successes. Or failures, come to that. But when they are in your classroom, you have been handed the baton of their learning and you must do something with it. Be bold. Give them the opportunity to LEARN.

The universe is full of magical things patiently waiting for our wits to grow sharper.

Eden Phillpotts, author and playwright

Class rules

This class is different. You get to make up your own rules. In pairs come up with your ideas for the following:

When I am talking to the class, I would like everyone to . . .

When I am trying new ideas, I would like everyone to support me by . . .

If I make a mistake, I want this to happen . . .

If there is a disruption in the class, I think the best way to handle it would be to . . .

So I can do my best work, I like to see, hear and feel these things around me:

I can best help my classmates by:

Ways to get the students to generate their own learning

- 5 mins writing down their own ideas about how to approach topic, then 5 mins in pairs to produce a combined list.

- Work in pairs to discuss and decide on the three most important factors about the topic.

- Work in pairs to discuss and decide the three questions that need answering on the topic.

- Class map of the topic; students to use post-it notes to write their questions and ideas which are then categorised and placed as a diagram on a wall or window.

- Each student to research a piece of info for next lesson – randomly allocated.

- Each student to research a piece of info for next lesson – deliberately allocated.

- If students know their own Gardner intelligence(s), they opt to research info based on their preferred intelligence(s) and then disseminate it to the class.

- Get students to link their interests with the topic in some way: chemistry to horse-riding, numeracy to playing the guitar, history to Xbox.

- Give them just one or two words and let them come up with their own understanding, e.g. tsunami.

- Students to create a slide-show presentation showing the major points of the topic as if they were teaching younger students.

- Class to develop newspaper articles and TV reports about the topic as if it were breaking news.

- Students to debate aspects of the topic but have to be either a politician or a lawyer so knowledge and professionalism are key.

- Students to write a play or drama about the topic and then perform it.

- Students to construct an encyclopaedic entry about the topic collecting all the information known, including required prior knowledge, glossary and information still needed.

- Design a virtual field trip to study topics and concepts to be learned based on the content of the chapter.

- Students to research experts in the topic and invite them to visit their classroom or Skype. If not possible, students can supply own questions to be answered.

- Students to invent experiments connected to the topic; these can be social as well as scientific.

- Cover the walls with essential questions about the topic, challenge another class or teacher to a quiz.

Research and report game

Start a feedback session when everyone has to find out an interesting fact about a specific topic and briefly feed it back. The trick is not to get the same piece of information as anyone else, which encourages creative and wide reading. One point for a fact, two points if no one else has it. Keep a running score each week!

Tips and starter sources of information can be supplied that anyone can access via a library or the internet. Tips on how to encourage creative thinking can also be given. For example, students could:

- Draw up a thinking map about the topic to help them to consider a range of angles.

- Use word games to think of unusual combinations, e.g. the topic is ox bow lake formation and the first three words on this online word generator (http://www.wordgenerator.net/random-word-generator.php) were 'practical', 'lobe' and 'duckweed'. Try to make a connection.

- Find an expert on the topic, either in a book or online, or even send them an email. Ask them for their ideas.

- See if YouTube has any useful videos.

- Link topic with other school subjects, e.g. ox bow lakes seen through the eyes of Art or Maths or Languages, etc.

- Evidence and sources of facts *have* to be retained in case anyone challenges the fact as incorrect, or even made up!

This activity also links with marketing your subject as students generate their own lines of interest and engage in wider reading.

CHAPTER

4

Get real

Covering these topics:

Getting out of the classroom
Energy levels
The review habit
Success and Failure

How often do we treat young people as if our time with them is the most important thing in the world?

Ian Gilbert, *Essential Motivation in the Classroom*

Ahh. My favourite subject: The Real World. A place we often mention to our students, talk about in terms of skills and exam results and point to as if outside the school doors. I even go there myself sometimes.

I've often heard teachers say: 'If we're not preparing our students for the real world, then what are we doing?' In fact, according to Ian, on average students only spend a tiddly 15 per cent of their young lives in school so really they are spending the vast majority of their lives actually *in* this real world that we tell them about. What then can school teach our young people that they are not already experiencing for themselves? Well, apart from an appreciation of numerous different subjects and a variety of different social skills and conventions, school is actually the perfect place for our students to *step away* from the real world. I wouldn't go so far as to make a comparison with a health farm, but school could be a place where, for a few hours, the real world is suspended and an individual might experience some relief from the pressures of everyday life. A place where the world can be seen in perspective and useful techniques, strategies and tools about how to manage life can be learned. And it is this aspect of schools and teaching that keeps me fascinated year on year.

When we talk to our students about the real world, we really mean the real world that they will inhabit some day, when they are fending for themselves as adults. So really we are talking about their future with all its complications and possibilities, a real world that doesn't exist yet, and what we need to show them is ways to prepare for it.

One of the most useful ways to demonstrate how their real world might look is to get them out into one of our real worlds. It really is worth your time and effort to make contacts and networks as you never know you might find someone in business who might want to work with you further and bring an added dimension to the whole school.

Take some time out to sit down with your subject colleagues or pals in other subject areas and have a focused session on 'how to get more of out there in here' and brainstorm to your heart's content. If you work with other people on this, then there's a chance they'll be happy to split the work of actually picking up the phone and making the contacts with you. One contact made can equal hours of payback in terms of pupil motivation and understanding. Here are some ideas to kick off your brainstorming (if you'd like this in more of a checklist format, then please find *Real world possibilities* on pages 68–69):

Take them out:	Get them in:
Historical buildings and places	Local businesses
Galleries and museums	Large employers
Theatres and cinemas	High profile employers
Woodlands and forests	Parents and family connections
Beaches and fields	Small business owners
Hills and mountains	Local people with hobbies and interests
Houses and castles	Professional experts
Farms and zoos	University professors, doctors and lecturers
Parks and adventure challenges	Friends and personal contacts
Caves and tunnels	Representatives from trade organisations
Canals, railways, ports and airports	Careers and coaching specialists
City centres or the middle of nowhere	Retired people
Disused industry and brownfield sites	Councillors and MPs
Businesses in action: retail, banking, farming, etc.	Faith leaders and practitioners
Community centres, retirement homes, nurseries	Former students and teachers
Everyday streets and places around school	Teachers within the school
Educational and outdoor centres	Older kids within the school
Libraries and public buildings	Celebrities (worth a try!)

Again, what you are trying to do is fire up your students' imaginations and help them hook on to whatever your topic is. A new place or person may well be the very hook they need. Also, don't just think of where to go in terms of your subject area; we remember best what we think about most. So if you can make the memory *memorable* enough, the learning will stick. How about:

- Maths on a farm
- Spanish in historical buildings
- Physics at a brownfield site
- English literature in a forest
- Business Studies on a canal
- Music in a cave.

I know, I know, you want to think up some of your own. Be my guest . . .

It is also possible to make an impact in your lessons by getting someone in. Make use of your own contacts, council education departments or local education business partnerships if you have any. A great website for getting the working world into your classroom is Inspiring the Future; it's free to use and you could get your hands on all sorts of people in a variety of work roles, offering different perspectives on what they do and why. There are quite a few really quite high profile businesspeople on there too if you have a hunt around. Again, don't always assume you have to use your local bank manager to just talk about finance and money. One enterprising school booked a number of local business volunteers for the day and stationed them in a central location. Then, during the day, different classes visited them for different sessions: younger students had a *What's My Line?* Q&A type activity and older ones more specific careers talks. One year group interviewed each of the volunteers for articles in the school newsletter and the group even had a visit from an art class who wanted to practise their portrait sketching.

Take them out, get them in. It doesn't matter which approach you adopt; just keep exposing your students to new and exciting things, or the same old stuff but in new and exciting environments, so they learn to associate learning with excitement and discovery.

And while we're on the subject of exciting your classes, perhaps now would be a good time to reintroduce Ian's wonderfully apt fartlek, fartlek being not only Swedish for 'speed play' but also a great word to get your students' attention and teach them something they might find useful. More often used in the world of sports training, the idea of fartlek is that you do high intensity training, but intersperse it with lower level activity periods, the low level activity being just as important as the high intensity training. Back in the classroom this can be reproduced by changing the pace of teaching and learning. Ian suggests you pay careful attention to the energy levels required in each session you teach and make sure there is a mix of high and low level energy activities built in. The low level activities allow for a period of mulling, or to give it a more scientific name 'the reminiscence effect'. That is the time after learning has occurred that the brain uses to make meaning of it and store it in an appropriate place. Cramming too much learning into a short session either compromises the making sense part or the learning part, you choose. Or choose to fartlek more in the class.

The two-point perspective lesson on page 31 demonstrates a variety of energy levels at work, with the student being the one who selects the level of energy according to how they like to spend their time. Some will want to repeat the learning over and over; some will want to move about to help anchor what they are thinking about; some will want to talk it through with a friend. The types of activities are selected according to how much learning the students need to assimilate; sometimes the activities on offer might all be quiet and reflective and sometimes the students may need something more physical to get the blood flowing to the brain. Again, don't forget your students' many different ways to process information. After an intense period of study a physical type activity is often useful and welcome, but for some students just getting outside, breathing deeply or looking at the sky might be enough. The whole-class game of British Bulldog you planned may not be that productive.

This brings us nicely back to something I lightly skimmed over earlier. Did you spot it?

> 'the reminiscence effect'. That is the time after learning has occurred that the brain uses to make meaning of it and store it in an appropriate place.

It's the *in an appropriate place* part that is important. As I said a few paragraphs back, 'We remember best what we think of most'. OK, so that could be the words to a song that's been going around in your head, OR you can put this amazing capacity to work by applying a simple review cycle:

Review the learning:	Length of time required:
As a summary at the end of the lesson	A few moments to review the main topics
After 24 hours	Review main topics
After one week	Four or five minutes
After one month	Three or four minutes
After six months	As much as needed
Revise periodically	As much as needed

Learning to review and, ultimately, the revision process itself are pretty much as important as the information and learning in the first place. Remember Mr Pareto? We must make an effort to ensure more than 20 per cent of the information sticks. I was never taught how to revise, or perhaps I wasn't listening at school that day. Either way, I thought that if the information I was learning hadn't gone in and stuck in my head, then it wasn't going to make any difference re-reading it before the exam. It's sad to look back on that time and realise how utterly wrong I was. And how, with a system and a bit of effort, I could have learned a useful aspect to learning that is: *actually remembering what it is you have learned.*

Many, many years later I read the (fabulous) book *Mindset* by Dr Carol Dweck and was almost reduced to tears. Inside I recognised myself as someone who had never been taught the tools and, more importantly, *the reason* I should learn to apply myself at school. I had emerged from mandatory schooling with the fixed mindset that organised learning was not for me and that I'd be fine getting by on my hit-and-miss approach to information acquisition. This was still very much in evidence during my Arts degree show, which prompted the external assessor to comment: 'You really didn't go for it, did you?' No I hadn't 'gone for it'; I didn't know how and didn't think I was the kind of person who could anyway. It was only years later while reading Dr Dweck's book that I realised the full enormity of what had happened and how it *really* was. So I'm not going to let that happen to anyone else and neither are you, right?

Remembering to make time for remembering, so to speak, can be a little complicated and daunting but with a few organisational tools (for those that like them) or a system (likewise) it can become a nicely ingrained habit. Ooh, we're coming to habits soon, stay tuned. Until then see how much you can help students in your classes by building quick review periods into your lessons. Ian mentioned a school where they actually organised the start of each lesson so that the class reviewed what had been learned in the lesson prior. Although that sounds a logistical nightmare, it can be easily achieved by jotting down learning points to be reviewed and sending them over with a compliant student. This also works best with compliant colleagues. Probably best attempted with Key Stage 3 as it's clearly not going to work too well with mixed or streamed classes.

For light relief and to get your students in the mood, there's a great 'pro boffin' video made by students at John Paul Stevens High School, Texas, in the online resources. Some classes BEG to have it played as a treat!

And now it's time for another little note about habits. As mentioned earlier, habits are necessary for us to operate as effective human beings. If we started every day by wondering how to walk or open the fridge, I don't think we'd have progressed too far as a species. The human brain loves to create habits and so falls upon them like long-lost relatives and welcomes them into our lives. And, like certain long-lost relatives, having certain habits in your life may not necessarily be a good thing. More about habits in Chapter 5, but right now, needless to say, having a review habit is not such a bad thing for your students so feel free to put a few habitual review sessions into your lessons and encourage them to build review habits into their studies. *The review habit* on page 70 suggests an approach that might be useful to start with until the process becomes more natural.

There's nothing artificial about the process of the review habit. It does actually mimic the natural way we learn everything: practising until we know it. What is artificial is learning so many things at one time in an unnatural environment, like a school. The rhythm of knowledge-then-practice is disturbed because so much is required of us. It's certainly not impossible to learn huge amounts of knowledge, especially as the task of finding food and shelter should largely be taken care of by somebody else; it just requires a more conscious approach these days.

An interesting model of teaching and learning using a reality angle is outlined in *Creating Outstanding Classrooms* by Oliver Knight and David Benson. They propose to start at the very top of the learning tree, at PhD level, and bring the essential strategies for acquiring knowledge back down to Key Stage 3 and carefully consider what skills and competencies needed to be achieved at each level. They refer to the process of looking towards the highest level first as 'playing the whole game' as it is only when students understand the mastery of the whole game, presented in a level-appropriate version, that they can understand where they need to go. Knight and Benson offer 'The Fertile Question' as the starting point of each lesson, that is: a carefully constructed 'problem' that needs to be solved rather than a series of questions that need answers. They offer six principles of what makes a good fertile question. It must be:

- open – with several different solutions, not one fixed answer

- undermining – casting doubt on the learner's assumptions

- rich – requiring deep and widely useful research

- connected – relevant to the learners and the society they live in

- charged – with challenging ethical dimensions

- practical – it can be researched to a sufficient level using available resources.

Later in the book Knight and Benson tackle other issues, including assessment models, so, all in all, a worthy addition to the staffroom bookshelf.

Here's another, less intense, approach to preparing for the real world that requires conscious, even daily, application. Using research done in *The Unemployables* by Chris Lewis, Ian presented students with this tantalising checklist of qualities needed to succeed in business:

- determination

- creativity

- self-belief

- bravery

- positivity

- sheer energy.

He would then ask students to give themselves a score out of ten for each quality, then add up the scores for an overall 'employability score'. If you want to try this approach, check out *Success qualities* on pages 71–72. By looking at the lowest scoring qualities, you can encourage the students to think of ways to improve them. Here are some suggestions to start your students thinking about activities that might improve each quality:

Determination	Creativity	Self-belief
Perfect a skill	Learn new creativity skills	Review your successes
Beat a personal best	Make all your presents for Christmas this year	Practise feeling good
Overcome a fear		Overcome internal negative talk
	Don't stop at the first solution to a problem	

Bravery	Positivity	Sheer energy
Try something you have always avoided	Deliberately see the bright side	Start a sport or exercise
Face situations you don't like	Don't spend time with people with negative attitudes	Research and eat energising foods
Learn calming techniques	Don't watch the news	Get to bed early

There's an exercise on page 85 called *Model behaviour* and it shows a method of getting experts, famous people from history and celebrities to help you overcome issues and build skills and self-esteem. Pop over now if you can't wait to look, but come back afterwards as I want to tell you that it's a great exercise to use to help develop a high employability score. And don't worry if the employability score only rises slightly or not at all at times; it's the knowing you want to improve and working on it that's important. After all, in a society where 80 per cent (that number again!) of people don't set goals, if you're setting goals, you already have an advantage.

But what if you're setting these goals and not achieving them? Fantastic, I say. Well done and congratulations! If you're experiencing failure, then you're in great company. If you're experiencing failure and yet you still keep on going, you could be heading for the hall of fame:

- Theodor Seuss Geisel, AKA Dr. Seuss, had his first book rejected by 27 different publishers. His books have now sold over 600 million copies.

- Sir James Dyson went through 5,126 failed vacuum prototypes. He is now worth an estimated $4.5 billion.

- Albert Einstein did not speak until he was four and did not read until he was seven, causing his teachers and parents to think he had special needs. He later went on to win a Nobel Prize and change the face of modern physics.

- Thomas Edison was fired from his first two jobs for not being productive enough, although his 1,000 unsuccessful attempts at inventing the light bulb might suggest otherwise.

- Michael Jordan missed more than 9,000 shots in his career, lost 300 games and completely messed up 26 potential game-wining shots. He is considered one of the best basketball players ever.

- Bethany Hamilton had her arm bitten off by a shark at 13. Two years later, after an amazing comeback, she won the Explorer Women's Division of the National Surfing Championships.

- Colonel Sanders was 65 years old and broke. He offered 1,009 restaurants his secret chicken recipe before he got his first yes. There are now more than 18,000 KFC franchises across the world.

- J.K. Rowling was surviving on government benefits while her first book was rejected by 12 publishing houses. Can you believe she's now richer than the Queen?

- Henry Ford failed twice to launch his business and then endured losses of $50 million before the Ford Motor Company became one of the world's largest and most profitable companies.

- Sylvester Stallone had a troubled childhood and was expelled from 14 schools but found his passion in acting and has been at the top of the Hollywood game for nearly 40 years.

There's also an accompanying worksheet called *Famous failures* on page 73 that covers these stories.

In fact, reading all that makes you start to feel sorry for the following kind of people:

> There is a particular group that may leave school without ever having fully developed these life – and life-saving – skills and for whom the whole concept of failure is something strange and foreign to contemplate. We call these poor children 'more able' students.
>
> Ian Gilbert, *Essential Motivation in the Classroom*

We must build in opportunities for our more successful students to be challenged and to fail. These individuals, though talented, also need to build up resilience and mental toughness, ready for those moments in life when everything isn't happening so easily for them. Time to put up that Jean Piaget poster (online resources).

You could also do well to offer all of your students a leaf out of a book from the world of sales. Many theories of success have emerged from sales-orientated businesses where getting a prospective customer to say 'yes' can be so hard and yet so lucrative. I had a friend who once worked in telesales for a double glazing company; as you can imagine, this was not an easy environment. This was compounded by the methods practised to support the sales team: the manager simply handed a page torn out of the phone book to each of the sales staff and told them it was their 'calling list'.

My friend was expected to call each of the people on her page of the phone book to ask if they would be interested in a double glazing special offer. This obviously isn't an acceptable way to make sales now and, unsurprisingly, wasn't any more popular back then. My friend and her colleagues were subjected to anger, rudeness and worse when they made each call, but they kept on going because it was what my friend called a 'numbers game'. Sooner or later someone would say yes and they'd make an appointment for a double glazing salesman to drop by. The 'yes' happened roughly one in every 100 phone calls so all my friend had to do was to call 100 people and, chances are, she'd get a sale in one of those calls. As their wages were based on commission from sales, they tried to get through as many of the no's as possible, because they knew that sooner or later a yes would happen.

If you are trying to do something but keep failing and getting knocked back, how many times do you think you would keep trying before you gave up? Entrepreneurs like Richard Branson, Duncan Bannatyne and Donald Trump all said they would never consider giving up – they would keep on trying, no matter what. And they did. Wouldn't it be great if you never feared failure but took it as a sign that you were getting nearer to success? How would it feel if you noticed other people giving up when they could succeed at something but you found you could just keep going and trying again and again? How brilliant would it be to not understand why anyone would want to give up on something they wanted and, as a result, you always achieve everything you want to?

So if failure is a great thing to get familiar with, then why not practise failing as often as possible? How about setting your students a task to invent a game where repeatedly failing is the main objective? This gets them comfortable with the idea of talking about failure and it being a part of the exploration and growth in life. Here are some ideas to get your cogs whirring:

- The game can be based on something that already exists, like Draughts, Ludo, Cranium or Jenga.

- Make up a whole new game that rewards the players who keep going even after they have had lots of setbacks.

- An endurance game where the last person still playing at the end wins.

- A game where you have to have failed at something to progress further.

- A verbal game where you have to remember times when you have made mistakes; extra points for extra huge gaffes!

As ever, if you get the students to do the thinking, they'll come out with the most amazing ideas.

So, is there a way of training yourself so that you can handle failure better? Like a Losers' Gym or something? Well, multiple failures are good training or, if there's no time for that, you might want to have a go at rejection therapy. And if you've never heard of rejection therapy, here's the guy to show you how it's done: Jia Jiang. He wanted to get better at handling rejection and discovered the idea of rejection therapy. He set himself the task of being rejected 100 times so that he could get used to it and not fear it so much. Try searching for 'Jia Jiang' or go straight to the best bits via the online resources.

Failure is something that happens to everyone sooner or later in life. People tend to see failure as a bad thing but failure is only bad if it dissuades you from trying again. As we have seen, some of the most successful people have failed over and over again and nobody, I repeat NOBODY, who has got somewhere in life has avoided feeling a failure at some point. Notice I said *feeling* a failure not *being* a failure. And while we're celebrating failure as an opportunity to grow, that's all very well and good inside your classroom, but what happens in the rest of the school? How do the students talk to each other? How do the staff talk to the students? How do the staff talk to each other? Is there a whole-school movement that celebrates failure as growth? Do teachers routinely stand up in staff meetings and talk in glowing terms about what they learned during their disastrous lesson with 10B? No, I didn't think so. The whole tone of the school is set by the head teacher and when the head teacher decides that failure is to be positively discussed and *actually does this themselves*, then the staff and students can relax and get on with the business of learning and growing. You know what you have to do people . . .

The final part of this chapter links back to goal setting again. For anyone who tried the exercise *Goal setting made simple* on page 23 there is an extra bit that might be useful to consider. If you remember, computer scientists Allen Newell and Herbert

Simon defined intelligence as a set of steps. Let's look at those steps again, a little more closely:

1. Specify a goal.

2. Assess the current situation.

3. Notice how it differs from the goal.

4. Apply a set of operations to reduce the difference.

If, at step 3, we notice our progress is not taking us towards our goal, then we need to concentrate on step 4: identifying actions that move us back in the right direction. What we are doing here is demonstrating an *active* goal-setting process, one which encourages frequent assessment and action. Working with the goal setting to do with employability skills in this chapter, Ian suggests students should be encouraged to think back every night and assess what *specifically* they did that day to bring themselves closer to their goal. Take even a tiny step each day and the journey shall be completed and, once again, the power of incremental change is demonstrated at its most powerful and transformative. For those who would like a worksheet example for their students, please see the exercise *What did I do today?* on page 76. Once your students get into the habit of asking themselves 'What did I do today?', it can be part of a more reflective process. I'd say it's always best to write it down though, as sometimes it's really useful to see how far you've come.

Remember Art Williams and his wonderful 'do it' speech on page 13? Well, listen to him when he says:

> I'm not telling you it is going to be easy, I'm telling you it's going to be worth it.

And there's a funny little *Do it* exercise on page 75 looking at putting off things. Talking of which: how did you get on with the new skills you are being challenged to learn from page 29? You remember, those tasks your students are setting you? Oh, not done that yet? Well, don't forget that when your students watch you going through the process of challenging yourself, trying new skills and accepting the inevitable setbacks and failures, you are modelling an excellent example of how to handle these situations. Be sure to let them see as much 'warts and all' failure as you can (possibly tone down the expletives a tad) and show how failure simply informs you of a strategy that doesn't work. So move on to try to find one that works. I know it's a bit of fun but you never ever know what's going to cause inspiration to spark in a student's imagination. And you must never ever give up trying to cause that spark to ignite.

> Life is infinitely stranger than anything which the mind of man could invent.
>
> Arthur Conan Doyle

Real world possibilities

For those of you who love a checklist, have I got a treat for you.

Here's all you could want in a list to kick-start your thinking about getting your class and the real world to meet. Use it, make your notes and enquiries, then MAKE IT HAPPEN.

Take them out:	How could it link to learning?	Contacts and notes
Historical buildings and places		
Galleries and museums		
Theatres and cinemas		
Woodlands and forests		
Beaches and fields		
Hills and mountains		
Houses and castles		
Farms and zoos		
Parks and adventure challenges		
Caves and tunnels		
Canals, railways, ports and airports		
City centres or the middle of nowhere		
Disused industry and brownfield sites		
Businesses in action: retail, banking, farming, etc.		
Community centres, retirement homes, nurseries		
Everyday streets and places around school		
Educational and outdoor centres		
Libraries and public buildings		

Get them in:	How could it link to learning?	Contacts and notes
Local businesses		
Large employers		
High profile employers (high street banks etc.)		
Parents and family connections		
Small business owners		
Local people with hobbies and interests		
Professional experts		
University professors, doctors and lecturers		
Friends and personal contacts		
Representatives from trade organisations		
Careers and coaching specialists		
Retired people		
Councillors and MPs		
Faith leaders and practitioners		
Former students and teachers		
Teachers within the school		
Older kids within the school		
Celebrities (worth a try!)		

The review habit

Getting into a regular habit of reviewing what you have learned makes revision a doddle and can increase the ability to remember things by as much as 400%! Use a different sheet for each subject and don't forget to make a note of the dates in your dairy.

Subject				Date period of study	
Lesson date ——▶					Tick when done
Content of lesson ——▶					
Date for next review – 24 hours					
Date for next review – 1 week					
Date for next review – 1 month					
Date for next review – 6 months					

Subject				Date period of study	
Lesson date					Tick when done
Content of lesson					
Lesson date					
Content of lesson					
Date for next review: 24 hours					
Date for next review: 1 week					
Date for next review: 1 month					
Date for next review: 6 months					

Success qualities

Think of a brilliant example of when you demonstrated each of these qualities.

Determination
Creativity
Self-belief
Bravery
Positivity
Sheer energy

Today, how much would you score yourself out of ten for each of these qualities?

Determination	
Creativity	
Self-belief	
Bravery	
Positivity	
Sheer energy	
Add them up for your total employability score:	

Which one of your qualities would you like to improve?	
Think of four things you could do to improve this score. Ask others for ideas too.	
1	2
3	4

Which one are you going to do?	When?

Did you complete your task? What happened?

Your score before: Your score now:

What are you going to do next?

Famous failures

Can you match the person to their setbacks and failures?

Thomas Edison
Michael Jordan
Dr. Seuss
J.K. Rowling
James Dyson
Bethany Hamilton
Albert Einstein
Colonel Sanders
Donald Trump
Henry Ford
Sylvester Stallone

Missed 9,000 shots
Rejected by 1,009 restaurant owners
Had an arm bitten off by a shark
Didn't learn to speak until four years old
Had personal debts of $900 million
Expelled from 14 schools
Rejected by 12 publishers
5,126 failed inventions
Made a $50 million loss
Rejected by 27 publishers
1,000 unsuccessful inventions

By not giving up and continually applying themselves, what did these people then go on to do?

Thomas Edison

Michael Jordan

Dr. Seuss

J.K. Rowling

James Dyson

Bethany Hamilton

Albert Einstein

Colonel Sanders

Donald Trump

Henry Ford

Sylvester Stallone

Reflection on failure

Have you ever noticed that when things go wrong, it can lead to something even better?

Write about a time you failed to do something you really wanted to do:

How did you feel?

What did you do? Did you give up?

What happened as a result?

Do you still see what happened as a failure, or as something else?

Do it

Be like other successful people and keep doing whatever it takes until you succeed.

What is the one thing that you need to do to ensure success?

Why are you putting off doing this one thing?

What idea can you think of to help you get on with this one thing? You can ask someone else for their ideas too.

What's the best outcome if you do this one thing?

Why is this outcome so brilliant for you?

When are you going to do this one thing?

What happened when you did it?

Is it done now or do you need to keep on doing it?   Done now / Keep on

What did I do today?

My goal is:

Date:	What *specifically* did I do today to inch me towards my goal?

Get personal

Covering these topics:

Relationships
Helping students to be better people
Modelling success
The effect of society

I have met teachers fresh from college who are already so intransigent you could chain your bike to them. And, conversely, teachers who have seen many a summer holiday yet are still keen for new insights and ideas.

Ian Gilbert, *Essential Motivation in the Classroom*

You and I know that life is all about people.

People do business with people, make money with people, share ideas with people, sympathise and empathise with people, co-operate and collaborate with people. Learning to get on with others should be a curriculum subject in itself. But not to worry, our students have you on hand to demonstrate how it's done. Oh yes, eagle eyes are always watching and processing, after all they're in a professional workplace when they are at school and they will be keen to see how professional relationships are managed. From the head teacher's defeated slump as he addresses assembly, to heated discussions between staff, to the way you rolled your eyes when a colleague is mentioned; they see it all. But most of all they notice their own relationship with you, the way you greet them, address them and treat them. Like it or not, you are both in this relationship together. Treat it with care and consideration as it's a relationship that may last longer than you think. I once had a carousel timetable that meant I would teach the entire Key Stage 3 cohort over the course of a year plus my Key Stage 4 classes plus a stray art class I'd picked up. One year on and I had pretty much taught everyone on roll in that school. It was a whirlwind of new faces and classroom dynamics so I can't say I *knew* all of them, but that was 20 years ago and when I'm in that particular part of London I *still* get people coming up to me in the street and saying I was their teacher. What's clear is that they remembered our relationship so it seems I did OK managing that haze of student faces. We must not overlook the fact that we might have been or might still be an important person to our students and should treat that knowledge with the utmost respect. Whatever your creationist/evolutionist point of view, we are in the position of teaching our students simply because we are older. We got on the planet before them and, as a result of that simple fact, we happen to know more and have therefore become their teacher. One sci-fi twist in time and it could all have been so very different!

In Chapter 6 there are a number of ideas about how to make your herpetarium easier for its inhabitants, but much of what you can do relies on your relationships with your students and that is something you need to work on and invest time in. Silly question: do you know all of their names? Do you pronounce them correctly? I once scribbled basic notes about each student: small, curly hair, odd-looking eyes etc. help identify members of my new form class during registration. Worked brilliantly until the day we started with an assembly and I found myself staring in vain at the long line of unidentifiable profiles stretching away from me . . . ah yes, of course, students can sit sideways too. So, in essence, *notice* each of your students. Be kind to them, no matter how many of your buttons they might try to press. They, like you, are just working with what they've got and they may be having a life of terrible troubles, in which case you *do* want to help. You will want to be a kindly face in their day, someone they can joke with when the opportunity arises. Someone who understands them well enough to keep their comments out of the public arena when the homework looks like it has been done walking across the playground on the way to your lesson.

Oh, and while we're on the subject of kindness, nip to the online resources and find the Smile poster, print it out and get it up on the classroom wall. Even better, make your own giant one or, completely best of all, get all your students to make hundreds and plaster the school. We should all: Smile. More.

Smiling is the simplest, cheapest and best tonic out there. It warms and welcomes, diffuses tense situations, disarms belligerent colleagues and can bring about a marked improvement in your physiology in times of need. Even a fake smile can work wonders. In fact, the phrase 'fake it 'til you make it' is a useful one to recall at all times when dealing with trying classroom situations. At any given time you can appear confident, in control, happy to see your students and joyful in your choice of teaching as a career. You know, if you ever find you have to.

Also, for a fantastic way to have instant desirable attributes, check out the exercise *Model behaviour* on page 85; it's not just for your students to use. This particular exercise was developed from an idea used in Neuro-linguistic Programming, or NLP as it is more often called. NLP first came about in the mid-1970s when its founders Richard Bandler and John Grinder wrote a book detailing observations they had made about the language and behaviour of eminent psychologists and psychiatrists. Indeed, they modelled what they learned, called it NLP and it has since evolved into the sprawling multi-million-pound industry that we know today. Love it or not, NLP has many practical applications in the classroom and in the lives of your students. I have used the technique outlined in *Model behaviour* numerous times myself; if there was more space here, I'd tell you how I once manifested Carol Vorderman right in the middle of Curry's Electricals. I've also successfully used it while working with adults, especially those struggling with specific situations who feel powerless to change anything. It works. Have a go yourself and with your students.

The *Model behaviour* exercise is better as a solo one, but I have used a slightly different modelling approach for whole classes, with both awesomely effective and hilariously entertaining outcomes. Teach your students this technique and they will thank you for years to come!

First, get your class to decide on the problem that needs solving, for example:

- how to design a personal revision plan

- thinking up an enterprise activity

- how a volcano works
- organising school council elections.

After identifying the problem, get the class to brainstorm people who would be useful to advise them on the activity. They can choose people they know, people they have read about or seen on TV or characters in films. Generate a list, for example a class-generated list of people who could advise on how to design a personal revision plan:

- Harry Potter
- Charlie's friend Sam in Year 8
- Richard Branson
- Ms Dreyfus, maths teacher at school
- Lisa Simpson
- Ant and Dec
- Dede from TV show *Sadie J*
- Jamie Oliver

etc.

Next, arrange a chair as the hot seat, in clear view of the whole class. Tell the students that one of these people will be coming into the classroom to help them with their problem. Ask if anyone would like to pretend to be someone on the list and get them to sit in the hot seat and answer questions about how they would approach the problem. This exercise might possibly start slowly as the students get used to the role-play element, but when they get the hang of it the activity really takes off and can generate amazing insights.

The trick for this exercise is to advise the student in the hot seat not to rush to try to think of answers, but to 'step into' the role and spend a moment to really feel they are the person in question. Imagine how they hold themselves, the expressions on their face and how they talk. When the other students are asking questions, encourage the hot seater to relax and say the answers as they pop into their head. Some people can step into these roles really easily and others may take a few practice runs before they get confident at it. This can also be useful for brainstorming sessions and can be hugely entertaining, and informative, when someone really gets into their stride. It's like having that person in the room. If you hit a particularly theatrical seam within your students, you can get them to take on the roles of key characters in your syllabus: rulers, explorers, scientists, writers. Or mix it up a bit and have Henry VIII comment on Einstein's general theory of relativity. But then I would suggest that, wouldn't I?

This exercise can also be useful as a paired activity, the students taking it in turns to ask and answer the questions. This approach can sometimes be more effective for quieter students as they might be happier to take on a role-play activity with just a friend as a witness. Or they could report back what they think their character would have said, as in 'I think Lisa Simpson would approach designing a revision plan by . . .'. This activity can also be done as a solo exercise. Arrange a hot seat as before, imagine the person you want to help you is sitting in it and ask them a specific question that you need help on; then you go and sit in the chair and take on the role. It's a big old grown-up game of pretend and it can work like a charm with some very surprising results.

The next way we can be useful to our students is to stress the importance of keeping good company and that they should aim to collect a healthy community of friends and family around them. As we know, a supportive community can help and encourage individuals to reach for their dreams and be with them along the way, even when times are tough.

The exercise *A healthy community* on page 86 expresses attributes of a healthy community as described through an assortment of scenarios your students might have experienced with their friends. Alternatively, get your class to brainstorm their thoughts about what constitutes a healthy community. Their ideas might include:

- listening

- enough time for all

- positive, even when giving tough feedback

- able to make mistakes

- able to express all ideas and thoughts

- non-judgemental

- share with whole group, not cliquey

- ask for help when needed

- offer to help others

- share your knowledge and skills

- keep learning and bringing in new ideas and information

- understand all the members in the community and be sensitive to their needs.

Sad to say, but not everyone has access to such a supportive community and it is important to make it clear what an individual can do to find one. Again, the class brainstorm could elicit ideas such as:

- Ask a friend or family member to be more supportive and tell them the ways in which they can.

- Find a group that shares your interests and make friends within it.

- Only listen to the opinions of people who support you.

- Find a youth counsellor or mentor that you can rely on.

etc.

Equally sad to say that at this point you must also pass on the appropriate wisdom and warnings attached to seeking help in online communities, random adults other than in a trusted network and the various other nasties we have to contend with these days.

Here's something else you can tell them. As they get older, they will only really tend to hang out with people with the same views, ideas and (interestingly) relative wealth as themselves. So, therefore, they need to choose wisely who they spend their time with as these people are going to be the biggest influence on their lives and the way they think. So, if their friends study hard and expect to go to the top colleges and universities, so will they. If their friends are always thinking up ideas and schemes to make money, so will they. If their friends drink, take drugs and mostly bum around causing trouble, so will they. But of course mention that if at any point they want to be different, all they have to do is gravitate towards a set of people with the kinds of attitudes and ambitions they share and make some new friends there instead.

Right now though it could be that your students don't have many choices about who they hang out with. Family they really can't do much about (*that* never changes!) and friends will be largely connected with school and their local area. Oh and there's you of course. You are potentially a part of each of your students' communities. And there are lots of additional ways you can steer them on key matters in between imparting your knowledge of longshore drift or the finer points of bowling a bouncer. I'm not suggesting that you are adding anything not already covered by the mighty PSHE juggernaut, but that sometimes the information has to come from an additional source before a student can assimilate it. And that additional source might well be you, so the following ideas are nice tools that a young person could find useful. And easy for you to blend into everyday lessons.

A good place to start is to routinely focus your students' attention on what they are bringing into your class each time. The moods and feelings your students bring into your classroom cannot be easily overridden, and they are never just sat there like blank little slates waiting for information. And, no, we would not like it if they were. The exercise *How do I feel?* on page 87 is an excellent starting point and very easy to adapt to your classes. I wouldn't run it every session, but often enough so they get into a *habit* of associating you with this particular line of questioning and therefore begin to assess themselves as they walk in. There is more on associations like this in Chapter 6.

Once your students have identified the feelings they are bringing into the classroom, they can choose to channel them, change them or park them at the door and pick them back up again as they leave. Don't dismiss this last idea entirely; it works brilliantly with all ages, including adults. It's based on another NLP idea, that of 'stepping out'. You simply step out of the emotions and feelings and leave them where you can come back to them later. You're not dismissing the emotions, or suppressing them, you're just stepping away from them for a while so you can concentrate on something else. Funnily enough, some people insist on picking their emotional state back up again as they leave the room, and that's fine. Or give them the choice to leave it there with you while they go and carry on with their day.

Something that students often get a bit mixed up with is their emotional state and their physical state. For example, a student might complain of feeling down when in fact they may be tired or, more possibly, just lethargic. My first teaching job was in a boys' school where I learned a great trick to tell the difference between my students being sluggish and genuinely fatigued. As I noticed heads being propped up and attention wandering, I'd pipe up with 'Anyone fancy a game of football?' and watch alertness ping back into their eyes. While they didn't get their football game, they did benefit from the change of activity that ensued and I gradually got the idea of pacing my lessons better. Teaching students to identify when they have a lack of energy, especially when it's masquerading as something else, is an easy skill and you can start them off with *I have no energy* on page 88. Here they can look at strategies for snapping out of that self-induced listlessness brought on by what my mother would call 'drooping about' and will have a useful secret weapon for similar episodes throughout their lives. Also handy to inflict on their own children at some point.

If you don't get a chance to disseminate all this advice to all your students, then please consider making a special effort to get this last point over to that little buddy you're helping give a leg-up in life: 'It is easier to prevent bad habits than to break them.' This pearl attributed to Benjamin Franklin.

Beware though, a bit like when you try to explain the wonders of compound interest to some people they start to glaze over, mentioning the importance of establishing good habits can appear to induce a near comatose state. But it's all in the delivery and I think you might be the very person who can help dispel some myths and big up the magic of habits.

For a start, most people think that habits are something they don't want (nail-biting, comfort eating, visiting online casinos instead of paying the gas bill) or that they *should do* (exercise, save money, put that cream bun down). Very few people talk about actively cultivating good habits that you can actually tolerate. Take it easy, start small and build up to more ambitious habits as you feel you can. It is self-defeating to have huge ambitious goals that you repeatedly fail to achieve – same with habits; break them down into do-able steps. Want to run a mile each morning? Make sure your running kit is ready beside the bed as you turn in for the night. That way you can at least get into the habit of putting it on first thing. Then work on getting outside the door and you've 90 per cent nailed it. I'm serious. The biggest barrier to establishing a habit like that is waking up in the morning and telling yourself your kit's in the wash / too hard to search out / missing a vital component. And, while we're on the subject of putting up barriers, some people hide behind the fact that a habit takes at least 21 days to establish, so they decide in advance to give up as they know they won't stick at it. Actually this is wrong. The 21-day theory was originally taken from a study that a notable plastic surgeon, Dr Maxwell Malt, published in 1960. Dr Malt noticed that it took patients around 21 days to get used to their new face or a new situation like having a limb removed. It led him to conclude that 'it requires a minimum of about 21 days for an old mental image to dissolve and a new one to jell'. The book this statement occurred in was called *Psycho-cybernetics* and became an overwhelming best-seller, shifting over 30 million copies. Of course, fame like that means you're going to get attention. And also misquoted, as it turns out. So many influential people read Dr Malt's book and began talking about it that the original '21 days' quote was truncated more and more and began to be held up as proof that it takes 21 days for a new habit to form. That age-old game of Chinese whispers at work.

More recent studies say that habits might take as long as 66 days to become embedded. And yet other studies have shown it could take even longer; a hefty 254 days has been suggested. But I think habits probably take as long as you want to embed. If you believe the habit will be good for you and you want to do it, then you might pick it up straightaway and never look back. Let's be honest, if you don't really want the habit in the first place (going to the gym anyone?) then it might never stick. So I suspect it's got less to do with how many days and more to do with how much you want to do it. What we must make our students aware of is how their habits form *them* as people. Check out *Good habits bad habits* on page 90 for a bit of an eye-opener.

Organise your students to work either alone or in pairs at first to brainstorm bad habits that they might be aware of; also encourage them to think of things that might not at first *appear* to be bad habits like daily high intensity workouts. Or you could fill in the habits section on the table yourself to get students thinking about specific scenarios. Here are some starter ideas for bad habits:

- messing about in class

- not bothering to remember things

- not planning revision

- listening to music when studying

- texting / using Facebook when studying

- dismissing people who are different from you

- not bothering to wash or take care of yourself

- not bothering to write neatly or correctly

- not keeping your room tidy

- smoking

- not being polite

- always having an excuse for not doing something

- blaming others for your errors

- moaning when things go wrong

- expecting someone else to sort out your messes

- always taking the easy option.

The fun starts when you get them to imagine that habit sustained over ten years and the astonishing impact that incremental change can have. Encourage them to play out the scenarios to their fullest extremes. Perhaps then they might be keen to try to avoid the future of doom and start scribbling away and deciding what might be a better set of habits to acquire. If you fancy a quick illustration of habit compounding, then let's go to the oft-used comparison of our daily coffee stop. Now that many of us are living lives akin to the 1990s/2000s sitcom *Friends*, many people consider a daily stop at a coffee shop their treat or even their right as in I-work-hard-I-deserve-this. But if you changed *nothing else* but included a medium-sized cappuccino in your daily routine, then in a year you will have gained an entire extra stone in weight. Or 6.35 kg if you're metrically orientated. Oh and will have spent an extra £900 in the process. (All my own calculations and I have been generous in allowing you a take-out coffee each time, not a sit-in and natter like I know you enjoy sometimes, not to mention all the other edible bits and pieces you might also consume). Yes, I am aware that this is a slightly unrealistic scenario; however, the point I am making is sound: habits incur incremental change. And if I was *slightly* more unscrupulous I could well make a few quid selling an ebook entitled 'My secret method of dropping a stone and adding £900 to your savings within a year', or some such.

So habits are what we thrive on; it's just important to limit the bad ones and consciously create good ones that point towards your goals. Ian mentioned the great story about Charles Lindbergh which beautifully demonstrates how someone can systematically identify and then practise behavioural habits with a specific end goal in mind:

How to be the first to fly solo across the Atlantic

In the race to be the first to fly solo across the Atlantic in the first half of the last century, Charles Lindbergh showed he would do whatever he had to do in order to succeed and, at the same time, showed how malleable our personalities are if we have the desire to change.

In his book, *Charles Lindbergh – An Autobiography*, Leonard Mosley quotes Lindbergh as he drew up a list of rules to live by:

> 'I came to the conclusion that if I knew the difference between the right way to do something and the wrong way to do it, it was up to me to train myself to do the right thing at all times. So I drew up a list of character factors.'

Lindbergh identified sixty-five factors, including '. . . alertness, altruism, ambition, aptitude, balance, brevity, concentration, diligence, enterprise, foresight, honesty, intuition, judiciousness, manliness, orderliness, precision, quiet temperedness, reserve, solicitude, tact, usefulness, watchfulness, zeal . . .', which he then used to mould his personality in order to achieve his goal. As Mosley points out, 'He then changed from a quiet, taciturn, serious, solitary man to a convivial, hand-shaking one . . . but only if it brought him nearer to the attainment of his objective.'

This links in brilliantly with the modelling as described earlier in this chapter. By getting your students to study the people they admire, they can then identify the attributes they find desirable or useful to model in their own lives. It's also a very useful exerciser for empathy as you can really walk a mile in someone else's shoes via modelling in this way.

> I've learned that you can tell a lot about a person by the way he/she handles these three things: a rainy day, lost luggage, and tangled Christmas tree lights.
>
> Maya Angelou

Model behaviour

Fancy getting someone super-cool to help you out? Answer the questions below. You can choose from people in films or TV, real or fictional characters, people from history, sports heroes, pop stars, your friends, family or teachers. Whoever you think will do the job best! The first one is an example.

Who is the . . .	
. . . most confident person you know?	*E.g. Peter Jones from* Dragons' Den
. . . most confident person you know?	
. . . most stylish person you know?	
. . . happiest person you know?	
. . . most honest person you know?	
. . . most fearless person you know?	
. . . most entrepreneurial person you know?	
. . . wisest person you know?	
. . . calmest person you know?	

Use the modelling technique to get these people to help you when you need them. Step in and really feel what it must be like to be them. It may surprise you what you can do with all these amazing skills at your fingertips.

A healthy community

You have to think carefully when choosing who to hang out with. People around you have more influence on your behaviour than you think! See if you can spot which are the healthy and which are the toxic communities . . .

When you want to do something different for a change	
Your friends just walk off and do what they usually do anyway	You all do something different or one or two of your friends join you
When you tell them about your plans to be an airline pilot	
They just laugh and say you're too stupid and you'll never do it	They support you and help you plan how you are going to do it
When you are down and need cheering up	
Your friends take time to do something special to make you smile	Your friends carry on the same as usual
When you have a problem you need to discuss	
Your friend just wants to talk about themselves	Your friend sits and listens to everything you want to say and then helps you find a solution
When your friends are doing something wrong and you tell them	
They stop	They laugh at you and call you names
When you are doing something wrong	
Your friends think it's really funny and encourage you to keep going	Your friends tell you and want you to stop
When you have to get on with your homework	
Your friends call you a boffin and want you to come out with them instead	Your friends study with you or call you later when you have finished
Your friends	
Always want the best for you and for you to be happy	Criticise you and want you to do what they want to do

Come up with more examples of healthy and toxic communities. Test your friends to see if they can tell which is which.

© 2015 *A Teacher's Companion to Essential Motivation in the Classroom*, Georgia Holleran and Ian Gilbert, Routledge

How do I feel?

Coming into school/class today I feel:

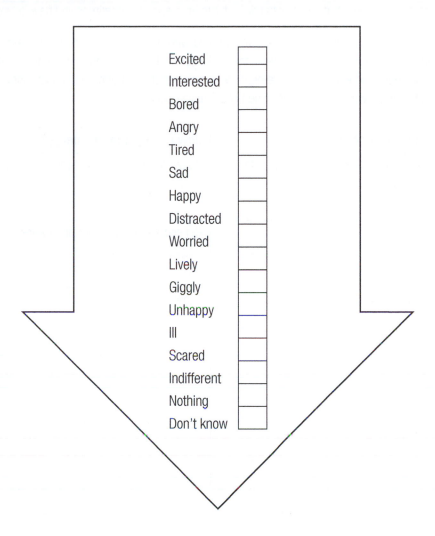

Excited

Interested

Bored

Angry

Tired

Sad

Happy

Distracted

Worried

Lively

Giggly

Unhappy

Ill

Scared

Indifferent

Nothing

Don't know

How will my mood affect my
learning today?

What strategies can I use to maximise my learning today?

- Talk about my problems
- Write my problems down
- Park my problems at the door

I have no energy

Do you sometimes just sit there, with loads of things you have to do, but you just feel you don't have the energy? Everyone does from time to time but, guess what, in order to have energy sometimes you have to *expend* energy.

People who run seem to have more physical energy. People who dance like scalded cats seem to have more energy. People who wave their hands around when they talk seem to have more energy. In each case it's because they are generating their own energy, by movement. Who ever heard of an energetic couch potato? So try this exercise to remind yourself what you could do when you feel you need a boost.

Times when I have no energy	How I can get more energy?
Watching TV all evening, falling asleep on the sofa	Go out for a brisk walk round the block
Feeling down	Get some loud music on and dance
Wake up and still feel sleepy	Shower!!

More examples of energy-bringing activities: laughing with friends / on the phone, looking up at the sky, taking deep breaths, vacuuming the carpets or cleaning the bath (believe me!), hula hooping / skipping / walking / running, singing out loud to an upbeat song (you could make a collection of them for times of need). Compare ideas with your friends; you'll probably end up with a huge long list.

But that's boring!

Want to know a strategy for when you're really not interested in learning something? Brainstorm all the different ways to learn and remember information and choose any number of techniques you'd like to try, or think of your own.

Draw a diagram	Make it into a song	Make it into a comic strip or storyboard	Use photos
Make it into a story	Draw a picture	Draw a map of the learning	Crib cards
Make a video	Use bullet points	Buddy up with a friend or group and each remember one aspect and then teach the others how they learned it	
Make it into a play	Test different memory techniques		

But don't do nothing. You have the responsibility for learning how to learn. So make it interesting for yourself, and make the learning stick!

Good habits bad habits

Are your bad habits really doing you no favours at all? Think about the consequences in ten years' time . . .

It's not too late YET. Make yourself some better habits now and harness the power of incremental change!

Bad habit	Consequence in ten years	Better habit
Staying up late playing games, online or watching TV	<ul><li>Will look older / tired</li><li>Will not have got the best grades due to tiredness</li><li>Maybe in low-paid job due to low grades</li></ul>	<ul><li>Get to bed early enough to get enough sleep – 8 hours</li><li>Do something peaceful like reading or listening to calming music so you fall asleep quite quickly</li></ul>
Not bothering to review lesson content regularly	<ul><li>Will not find revision easy</li><li>Will not get into a learning habit</li></ul>	<ul><li>Review what you have learned every day</li><li>Every night ask yourself the three main things you learned from each lesson</li></ul>
Leaving homework until the last minute		
Eating junk food		
Not taking any exercise		

Bad habit	Consequence in ten years	Better habit

CHAPTER

6

Reptiles in the classroom

Covering these topics:

Contain, Entertain, Explain
Habits and branding
Curiosity
Branding your lessons

Unless we emotionally believe something to be true, we do not fully believe it.

Ian Gilbert, *Essential Motivation in the Classroom*

In the last ten years studies exploring Mind, Brain and Education (MBE) Science have exploded in popularity, leading to a wealth of fascinating insights into how the brain learns. It may even be that the role technology plays in our lives is causing younger people's brains to be rewired differently from those of previous generations, in ways that are both good and bad for individuals and society. An epic book on the subject is *Making Classrooms Better* by Tracey Tokuhama-Espinosa, which leaves you in no doubt as to what (50!) teaching activities and strategies make a difference in the classroom. However, the sheer volume of information needs to be carefully managed so as to avoid 'info-swamp', so more of a summer holiday project read than a tea-break dip in. I have précised her, and other brilliant brain researchers', work here for the purposes of practicality but there are further resources and websites listed in the online materials for this book.

Never forget that you, as the classroom teacher, are still the single most important factor when it comes to learning, even when we're looking at learning through a 'pure biology' lens of brain function. Your *genuine* modelling of lifelong learning through enquiry, wonder and reflection speaks silent volumes to your students (and peers, should they be aware enough to pick up on it). And even the vocabulary you use reinforces your attitude to learning:

- Upon hearing some 'constructive' feedback: 'Oh thanks, I hadn't thought of it that way; next time I'll remember to consider that.'

- Encouraging team research in class: 'What a great question! How about we figure that out together?'

- Problem solving strategies: 'What do you already know that can help you resolve this?'

- Encouraging self-knowledge: 'Brilliant answer! How did you get that?'

As a teacher it would also be wise to consider key factors in the way the brain works, some of which are:

- The plasticity of the brain means that can influence our thoughts and actions **on an ongoing daily basis.**

- It is impossible for the brain not to learn. The key is to make that learning **interesting** to a student.

- Both of the facts above mean that it is imperative to keep on being interested in life and to learn, which actually **wards off the brain's perceived decline** in old age.

- **The brain wants to use what it already knows** to build ideas, connecting similar concepts and comparing old information with new.

- The brain enjoys novelty but **needs to detect patterns in information** to be able to notice when difference is occurring.

- **The brain processes information both in parts and as a whole, simultaneously,** as we subconsciously choose to 'hold' or 'use' new information accordingly.

- **We learn best through social interaction.** Even if we think we prefer to work on our own, we generally gain information and learn about ourselves by comparing our actions and thoughts with those of others.

Our friend Howard Gardner of multiple intelligences fame has, more recently, called for attention to be paid to the types of mind that may be most useful for us to develop in the future:

- The Disciplined Mind: a capacity for sustained and deep thought leading to mastery of a subject. Not be the jack of all trades that technology and life in the twenty-first century allow us to be.

- The Synthesising Mind: to be able to take data and experiences from diverse areas and formulate them into something new. Often the capacity for a mind to synthesise comes with age and experience.

- The Creating Mind: to understand the box well enough to think outside it. That is to know a subject well enough to recognise an original concept.

- The Respectful Mind: to accept that others are different, not illogical or wrong. True multiculturalism, including the understanding of class and position, can teach this wonderfully.

- The Ethical Mind: to be able to think about long-term consequences in all aspects of life, professionally and personally.

For a great exercise you might like to do with students or as an opener for an INSET session, have a look at the *Brain truths quiz* on page 98. The answers are at the end of this chapter.

Let's now get to the practicalities, starting with how your students feel before they have even entered your classroom. Are they coming in with baggage? How do they feel about being with you for the next hour or so? Where have they just come from? What comes next after you? How can you manage all these conflicting situations? Well, the answer lies in understanding more about the brains that are bumping around inside the heads of those students. You might be aware of the triune, or evolutionary, model of the brain, which has been around since the 1960s. Although considered by anyone working in the field of neuroscience as an oversimplified explanation of the human brain, this model is still useful as a light-hearted way of illustrating the basic workings of the brain and is especially helpful for young people trying to understand themselves better. The triune model describes the human brain in three parts, starting with the oldest part on the evolutionary scale: the 'reptilian brain'. This part is the most basic level at which our brains operate, it being concerned almost entirely with our safety and biological mission to procreate. Or as Ian memorably puts it:

> What does a lizard need to be able to do to live a fulfilled and productive life? Stay alive and try to have sex – there's not much to it really. Think of the lizard as having the intelligence of a typical undergraduate.

The next part of the brain to have evolved is the 'limbic brain', which works with emotions. This part of the brain is important for making long-term memories. Again, Ian's handy reminder is priceless:

> Think of the intelligence of a dog. It does all that a lizard's brain can but, in addition, experiences emotions. Yet it cannot do the crossword.

Finally, we get to the 'human' part of the brain: the neocortex. This is where our unique traits of speech, abstract thought and reasoning have evolved, thereby putting us theoretically at the top of the evolutionary ladder. The interplay between the limbic brain and neocortex is what we need to target for learning to be embedded in our long-term memories. Ian summarised a teaching approach to satisfy each part of the brain as: Contain, Entertain, Explain. But, hold your horses, you won't get very far unless the lizard brain is relaxed, so we have to address that first. As mentioned in previous chapters, you can do a lot to 'brand' your lessons and that can work wonders on the reptilian brain.

Contain: Without straying too far into the various theories about human needs, one of the most basic needs for a human is that of food and it is a truly heartbreaking reality that many children arrive at school having had little or no breakfast. Whatever the factors are that cause this to happen, it's clearly not a problem that is going away any time soon, yet so many barriers to learning are put up from a simple lack of food; poor concentration, misbehaviour, illness, tiredness and inability to grasp information can all stem from the overriding need to eat. The reptilian brain kicking in. I am not suggesting that it's your responsibility to make sure your students are fed but, with a little bit of creative thinking, maybe an adequate (and free!) breakfast club really can be organised at your school. Please don't think that it's someone else's responsibility; chat to the head, speak to local charities, church groups, rotary clubs, local businesses, especially catering, bakeries, supermarkets and shops. You *can* make a difference, maybe a huge, life-changing difference to someone. An amazingly far-sighted primary head teacher I know insists on a mid-morning toast break for everyone, staff and students alike. The little 'uns take it in turns to help prepare the snack, which includes a honey, peanut butter or Marmite topping. So many life lessons being taught with one simple act.

Another lizard concern that your students bring into the classroom is safety. Hopefully fatalities due to volcanoes, floods, avalanches and attacks by giant predatory kangaroos (yes, really) are rare among your student population but some will certainly be attending school with other, very real, fears: bullying, conflict at home, poverty or past traumas. A Somali boy I taught had little command of the English language but would draw me stick people with machine guns. Again you cannot gather up all your students in your nursemaid skirts to protect them, and nor would it be appropriate, especially if you are a macho PE teacher called Dave, but you can offer them a sanctuary while in your lessons. Be vigilant for any anti-social behaviour, isolated or withdrawn students or out-of-character behaviour and suggest the 'park your troubles at the door' exercise, as described in the previous chapter, to those who may be going through normal growing pains.

So with hunger and danger at bay, what else can you do? Aha, this is where the 'branding' comes in. And what I mean by branding is managing what your students think and feel about your lessons. Bit too Orwellian? Not at all. It's just a bit of packaging.

Kick off in style as they come into the room. Be at the door and welcome them in. This is a great time to use music as part of your brand. Something lively but light would be appropriate; you don't want to get them too excitable. In fact, music in lessons is a great pace changer and mood enhancer. And because now you can devise your own collection or, even better, fire up YouTube, you can interject music whenever you feel like it. Retro theme tunes are just brilliant for adding novelty; Chris Evans started this trend over 20 years ago. Or for some great anonymous peaceful tracks search YouTube for 'Wonderful Chill Out Music'. There are some other ideas in *Music in the classroom* on page 99 and if you want to choose music from the whole world, you will not get a better start than by searching online for the World Music Network; there's a link in the online resources. A great way to leave them with a positive memory of the lesson with your 'theme tune'. Choose an upbeat theme tune or popular song. You could even have them leaving with 'Teach Me How to Study' ringing in their ears; see online references for the link. See also the 'Independent Thinking' classic *The Little Book of Music for the Classroom* by Nina Jackson.

As your students enter the classroom, it could be seen as a great opportunity for a bit of messing about, but, wait, you have something ready prepared to get them settled and warming up. This can be a dingbat, anagram, word puzzle, riddle or other quick warm-up activity and demonstrates to your students that when they come into your lessons, you get them thinking right away. As an extra incentive, the best solvers of the warm up could choose the exit music, or class 'thinking' music that day – from a prepared list; we don't need any hardcore rap when trying to study economic migration. For great links to warm-up resources see the online references. With the food/safety issues contained and the routine of the lesson start soothing your students into a relaxed familiarity, you can now pass Go and move on to your lesson content.

Entertain: Dealing with the limbic brain. Ian quotes research where students are asked what they are looking for in a good teacher. The main attributes always seems to be a sense of humour and consistency. I see those attributes both pointing to the same thing: giving the student a sense of security. Often humorous people make jokes and take jokes because they are secure in themselves and have the ability to step back and have perspective on life. Notice I said *make* jokes and *take* jokes. Heavy sarcasm and poking fun at people are not the traits of a secure person. You have to be able to laugh at yourself too. Teachers who remain constant in their behaviour also display a degree of emotional stability and self-esteem. Along with these traits Ian suggests other elements in a lesson that could awaken the learning brain:

- suspense

- intrigue

- curiosity

- novelty

- surprise

- awe

- passion

- compassion

- empathy

- hitting goals

- discovery

- competition

- overcoming obstacles

- achievement

- a sense of growth.

So the trick would be to get some more of these fine elements into your lesson plans. If you like a checklist, try *Entertain* on pages 100–102. Here you can take any of the associated words and play with your lesson content, for example:

- composition using just glimpses of something

- photosynthesis using revelation

- quadratic equations using eavesdropping

- the properties of different materials via cliffhangers

- the introduction to new vocabulary with trickery.

As ever, I'm sure you get my drift.

You can also deepen your own understanding of any of the elements by focusing on it. For example, what does empathy mean to you? Are you any good at being empathetic? Do you even think it has value? Question yourself about your interpretations and assumptions and if you feel you want to dismiss an element because it's not your kind of thing, stop right there and ask yourself why. You could be missing a vital spark in your lessons, a spark that might trigger something in one of your students. Then be brave: do the very thing you don't want to do and pop that element into your next lesson. Something else to try if you're investigating some inner resistance: take a leaf out of the NLP modelling book and think of someone who epitomises that attribute and then 'step into' them and understand what they feel like. Pop back to page 78 to remind yourself how to use modelling if you need to get reacquainted with it.

Quick starter tips for 'entertaining':

- Unusual deadlines, e.g. 'You have 7.5 minutes starting from now' or 'At 2:17 p.m. we'll stop and look at everyone's ideas'.

- Throw in a curve ball, e.g. 'Let's have a quick-fire Q&A on the Great Depression, only I'll tell you the answers first and then you tell me the questions'.

- Suspense: 'Coming up in ten minutes the secret to getting an audience's undivided attention'.

- Overcoming obstacles: tell your own story; when were you up against something impossible? What happened? What did you learn?

- Listen to how the professionals do it. Radio and TV presenters have a whole host of tricks to keep their audiences from straying: regular features, running jokes, rollover competitions, etc.

Your mission is to evoke emotions. Emotions make memories and cause brains to allow information to stick. How can you connect your topics with these positive emotions?

Admired	Cooperative	Focused	Non-judgemental	Skilful
Ambitious	Courageous	Forgiven	Organised	Spirited
Amused	Daring	Friendly	Positive	Strong
Appreciated	Decisive	Gratified	Powerful	Successful
Assertive	Defended	Honest	Praised	Tactful
Assured	Delighted	Honoured	Precious	Thankful
Authentic	Dependable	Hopeful	Progressive	Thrilled
Balanced	Disciplined	Humorous	Qualified	Trust
Bonded	Dynamic	Independent	Recognised	Understood
Brave	Empowered	Influential	Relaxed	Unique
Brilliant	Energised	Innocent	Respected	United
Calm	Excited	Inspired	Rewarded	Unselfish
Capable	Exhilarated	Invigorated	Self-reliant	Valuable
Captivated	Flexible	Joyful	Sharing	Valued
Centred	Flowing	Light-hearted	Simple	Worthwhile

Explain: Well, we're at the neocortex now so you should be able to work directly with the reasoning, processing and understanding part of the brain. Nothing new for you to learn here; roam free in your own area of expertise.

Something worth noting at this point is when you might have a tendency to go 'a bit reptilian' yourself. Well, yes it might be a good idea to keep a stash of oatcakes in your drawer for hunger pangs but I'm referring to something even more threatening. At a meeting recently, assorted primary teachers and I were discussing a digital skills training course on offer. I was suggesting that maybe the teachers would like to bring a Year 5 or 6 student along too so that the burden of recall was spread over two people from each school. They could also use each other for back up when teaching the skills on in the classroom; that way nothing important would be overlooked. I was genuinely open-mouthed when several of the teachers thought that having a student along was a bad idea. One teacher went so far as to say she couldn't have a student with her as she had to be the 'expert' in the class. So, do you know what threatens you? Do you have to be the expert? Or perfection some way? At the risk of ruining your day with this observation, I would hazard a guess that, considering the learning environments away from school now, it would be almost impossible for you to know more about some subjects than your students.

The roles are changing, have probably already changed, but maybe you haven't noticed; the line between teacher and learner is more blurred and fluid than ever. If you are threatened by this, then it's time to have a stiff word with yourself and adopt the role of facilitator in the classroom. Look at it this way: you're still way more experienced in life than your students are. Skills of research, discernment, creativity, encouragement and a genuine joy of learning are what you are now in the business of imparting. Knowledge is freely available but your students are looking at you to see how to manage themselves through life. They can see when you are displaying reptilian behaviours, especially if you're brave enough to teach them about the triune model of the brain, so be aware of your own triggers and try to have a strategy in place to prevent them from spilling out. Yes, you're right; team meetings are a great place to spot reptiles in action. Be an observer, not the entertainment!

Oh, and if you're looking for the answers to the *Brain truths quiz*, they're all FALSE. None of the statements have been proven to be true and many of these 'neuromyths' have been circulating for years in an attempt to sell commercial programmes to line the perpetrators' pockets. To be a more discerning consumer of brain research, see suggestions for further reading and information in the online resources section.

> The lizard brain is not merely a concept. It's real, and it's living on the top of your spine, fighting for your survival. But, of course, survival and success are not the same thing.
>
> Seth Godin, *Linchpin*

Brain truths quiz

How much do you *really* know about your amazing brain?

Are these statements true or false?	
Learning creates new brain cells	
Most people use about 10% of their brains	
The best way to receive information is via your preferred learning style	
The brain is plastic for certain kinds of information only during specific crucial developmental periods	
Removing emotion from learning improves quality of thought	
Teenagers are irresponsible because their prefrontal cortex doesn't develop until their mid-twenties	
Environments rich in stimuli improve the brains of pre-school children	
The brain has an unlimited capacity for memory; forgetting is simply an absence of recall	
The brain and the mind are unconnected	
Humans can multitask	
Children are sponges and can learn foreign languages effortlessly	
Even when 'brain dead' you are still conscious	
Listening to classical music makes you cleverer	
Omega-3 and Omega-6 supplements improve academic achievement	
Language is located in the left brain and spatial abilities in the right brain	
Everything important about the brain is determined by the age of three	

Music in the classroom

For instant access, type straight into YouTube and leave only the sound on.

Famous classics:	
For calming down or entering the classroom	
Chopin – Nocturne Op. 9 No. 2	Lakmé – The Flower Duet
Bach – Air on G string	Giacomo Puccini – 'Coro a bocca chiusa' (Humming Chorus) from *Madame Butterfly*
Erik Satie – Trois Gymnopédies	Tchaikovsky – Waltz of the Flowers
Debussy – Clair de lune (piano music)	Ludwig van Beethoven – Für Elise
For livening up or exiting the classroom	
Holst – Planet Suite, Jupiter	Rimsky-Korsakov – Flight of the Bumblebee
Sergei Prokofiev – Dance of the Knights	Edvard Grieg – In the Hall of the Mountain King
Tchaikovsky – Chinese Dance, The Nutcracker Suite	Richard Wagner – The Ride of the Valkyries
TV and film classics:	
Peaceful	
Barrington Pheloung – theme from *Inspector Morse*	Mike Post ft. Larry Carlton – *Hill Street Blues* TV theme
Gallery music from *Vision On*	*Last of the Summer Wine* theme
Lively	
Elmer Bernstein – *The Great Escape*	*The Avengers*
Knightrider theme tune	*The Sweeney* – opening track

And of course you can NEVER go wrong with starting or ending any session with ***Happy*** by **Pharrell Williams**.

Don't forget to tell your students what the music is each time you play it. You never know, they might want to re-create the same atmosphere themsleves . . .

Entertain

Here's a checklist to add the entertainment factor to any lesson. Read all the definitions and related words – you never know where inspiration will strike!

Suspense
A state or feeling of excited or anxious uncertainty about what may happen

Confusion	Tension	Thriller	Uncertainty
Cliffhanger	Expectation	Disbelief	Prediction
Assumption	Chance	Interruption	Unfolding

Intrigue
Arouse the curiosity or interest of; fascinate

Complication	Conspiracy	Double-dealing	Plot
Trickery	Tantalise	Enchant	Inveigle
Dazzle	Hypnotise	Collusion	Trick

Curiosity
A strong desire to know or learn something

Interest	Investigation	Gossip	Specialist
Prodigy	Phenomenon	Searching	Questioning
Prying	Inquiring	Eavesdropper	Nosy

Novelty
The quality of being new, original or unusual

Freshness	Oddity	Innovation	Uniqueness
Unfamiliarity	Strangeness	Permutation	Transformation
The latest thing	Newfangled	Development	Diversion

Surprise
An unexpected or astonishing event, fact, etc.

Revelation	Wonder	Jolt	Bombshell
Abruptness	Miscalculation	Sudden	Startling
Unnerve	Decoy	Overwhelm	Bafflement

Awe
A feeling of reverential respect mixed with fear or wonder

Wonderment	Reverence	Shock	Admiration
Stunner	Daunt	Faze	Bewilderment
Bedazzle	Impress	Repress	Goose bumps

Passion
Strong and barely controllable emotion

Spirit	Intensity	Warmth	Fervour
Fire	Suffering	Flare-up	Crush
Weakness	Appetite	Fire in belly	Drive

Compassion
Sympathetic pity and concern for the sufferings or misfortunes of others

Humanity	Sympathy	Yearning	Generosity
Lifesaver	Encouragement	Support	Cheer
Compunction	Good will	Indulgent	Tolerance

Empathy
The ability to understand and share the feelings of another

Rapport	Warmth	Good vibrations	Appreciation
Recognition	Charity	Grace	Congruity
Like-mindedness	Sensitivity	Understanding	Affinity

Hitting goals
The object of a person's ambition or effort; an aim or desired result

Target	Intention	Objective	Destination
Mission	Values	Enterprise	Plot
Big picture	Duty	Belief	Endurance

Discovery
Find unexpectedly or during a search – divulge (a secret)

Encounter	Happen upon	Come upon	Exploration
Claim	Glimpse	Ferret out	Suspect
Locating	Detection	Determine	Progress

Competition
The activity or condition of striving to gain or win something by defeating or establishing superiority over others

Struggle	Tournament	Rivalry	Go for gold
Controversy	Match up	Counteraction	Challenger
Tug-of-war	Participants	Duel	Free-for-all

Overcoming obstacles
Succeed in dealing with (a problem or difficulty) – a thing that blocks one's way or prevents or hinders progress

Conquer	Weather	Vanquish	Survive
Rise above	Master	Reduce	Victorious
Outplay	Transcend	Wipe the floor with	Outclass

Achievement			
A thing done successfully with effort, skill or courage			
Masterpiece	Completion	Feat	Actualise
Effort	Talent	Bring about	Undertaking
Fact	Materialisation	Culmination	Opus

A sense of growth			
The process of increasing in size			
Rise	Beefing up	Boost	Surge
Proliferation	Stretching	Enrichment	Headway
Advance	Strengthening	Magnification	Boom

Motivation is a four-letter word

Covering these topics:

Self-esteem
Creativity and strategies
A Handbook for Life
Whole-school approach to essential motivation in the classroom

A computer game that lets you know a week later whether you have been blasted by the evil Krug would not be a bestseller.

Ian Gilbert, *Essential Motivation in the Classroom*

And here we are at the final chapter where all the loose odds and ends get tidied up and everything makes sense, just like in real life.

This last chapter is about HOPE and Ian poses the question:

What are you doing to manage and maintain high levels of hope in your classroom *despite the immediate evidence*?

And by that he means that we're not to write anyone off or dismiss someone because they really don't seem able to grasp what we're teaching. Every day is a new day and we can never guess what might be different today that suddenly sparks a, seemingly uninterested, student's imagination. We can't guess but we do have to keep on going, trying different things and giving hope. I know; it takes a huge amount of energy but it is this very energy that students need from you in the classroom. Like little vampires, they need the energy of life that we exude. They notice our passions and our enthusiasm, what lights up our eyes and what makes our souls sing. Forgive me for waxing lyrical but I honestly feel that if we're not the best possible examples of adults that we can be, then we don't have any right to be in the classroom. Harsh? Maybe, but we can all recall the dreary, been-in-the-job-too-long teachers from our own school days; you may even recognise some among your contemporaries. What message is that kind of teacher sending to their students? Never mind what impression that gives about that teacher's curriculum subject, what impression are they giving off about life as an adult? We're adults, we're a bit better practised in how the world works and can overhear the same teacher's moans and complaints in the staffroom and then shake our head and forget about them. If you're a child and this teacher is your class teacher, or subject teacher, you're going to hear a disproportionate amount of moaning and groaning about life. It has an effect. Going back to Chapter 3 (p. 49): are you a DDM or DMD? Get that poster up on the wall in the classroom and in the staffroom. I believe some people don't even know they're doing it.

Some years back I was asked to do some fairly demanding change work with a large group of senior managers in a council. I used emotional intelligence in the form of EQ (Emotional Quotient) assessments, among other tools and diagnostics, to build a comprehensive picture of each person's capabilities and strengths. During that time I observed first hand how, in some cases, emotional issues can dog an individual's life, right through adulthood. Because the emotional development of an individual is an important factor in how they see the world, I could help those individuals identify at which point their EQ had been affected and quite possibly what had caused it. A fair bit of emotional damage can be caused in childhood and I don't necessarily mean via deliberate physical or mental abuse as, amazingly, some people find their way through this kind of damage and still have a very healthy EQ score. Emotional damage can be caused by an innocent comment, a specific incident, a lack of adequate parenting, a large number of siblings, a lack of siblings or an individual simply being a very sensitive child.

I'm not saying that we can stop the damage happening. How we learn to deal with situations like these is what makes us human and therefore this stage of development is quite important. But what I am saying is that if we educate our students about emotional intelligence and how it affects them, they might gain an understanding about their own potential emotional issues. With understanding comes the choice to change these issues before they interfere with the rest of the student's life, perhaps even affecting their own children. Sobering.

Emotional intelligence is a fascinating subject to study and also rather vast so please don't feel weighed down at the thought of struggling through it along with everything else you have to do. It might help if I simplify matters here by saying that there are two key factors we need to focus on primarily, and a quick understanding of the EQ assessment process will explain why. Anyone undergoing an EQ assessment is required to answer a series of questions and the answers are then scored against a number of weighted criteria. When the data crunching has happened, the report comes back with scores between 1 and 10 for each aspect of emotional intelligence, the first two being the most important. They are:

- your regard for yourself
- your regard for others.

These two factors underpin the whole of the EQ framework, and working to improve them can cause significant and profound changes throughout all the other aspects.

I used to draw this diagram for my clients:

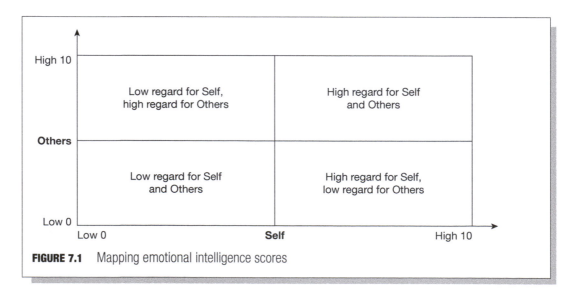

FIGURE 7.1 Mapping emotional intelligence scores

As I drew this for the client, I would explain that the first two scores on the EQ test could be plotted like co-ordinates and land them somewhere in one of the four boxes. For example a score of 2 for Self and 6 for Others would land them in the Low Self / High Others box. Depending on where their score landed them, I would then write in my *own, personal* descriptors and explain what each meant.

- Low Self / Low Others – I always said this was the 'Sadness' box as these scores meant this client had a low level of regard for anyone on the planet, including themselves.

- Low Self / High Others – This one I called 'Mummy' as it indicates someone who habitually puts others' needs before their own.

- High Self / Low Others – In my mind this is always 'Loadsamoney', based on the famous Harry Enfield character who thought he was better than everyone else.

- High Self / High Others – This I always refer to as the 'I'm OK, You're OK' box, from the book of the same name by Thomas A Harris and, obviously, the most desirable state to be in.

I must stress I used these descriptors only with my clients to help them understand the types of information that this part of EQ can give. They are most certainly not 'official' descriptors. Having taken this information in, the client would then invariably say one of two things:

'Is there any way in which I can improve these scores?'

'I wouldn't want to have a high score for Self because that would mean I thought I was better than everyone else.'

And the response to these two comments is why it is important that you have an understanding of EQ because:

You can *always* improve your regard for Self and Others.

Having a healthy Self score is *very* important indeed.

On that first point: yay, isn't it great news that we're able to improve our EQ? And on the second point: well, isn't that so very *polite* of us to not want to appear better than anyone else? Remember in Chapter 1 when the aeroplane was losing altitude and the oxygen masks dropped into the cabin? Altogether now: '*You put your own oxygen mask on first, before helping anyone else.*' In order to be any help to others, you have to be OK yourself. If you want to have a higher Self score, you are not saying you want to be better than others, you just understand how important it is to feel OK about yourself. 'Feeling OK about yourself' is more usually referred to as 'self-esteem'. And, as you know, an individual's self-esteem is pretty much key to how successful, and happy, they are in life.
So, here's the plan:

- You help your students improve their self-esteem.

- You help your students begin to understand that they deserve to have a high self-esteem and then they begin to understand that others do too.

I don't need to tell you that there's more than a few books, articles and websites out there to help you with the task of raising self-esteem in your students. Oh, and also making your students aware of what this mystical 'self-esteem' is and how its level can vary through the years depending on how life's situations are managed and handled. The practice of self-reflection can be useful for some people yet downright depressing for others; the trick is to reflect from the position of an observer, not a participant. Huh, Miss? Tell them to try to reflect on situations in their life as if they were an objective journalist writing for a newspaper, not a popular novelist squeezing the maximum emotion into every word. There are also a number of effective NLP exercises that can help you gain perspective. I've read many NLP books, but some do seem to get a bit bogged down in technicalities and vocabulary. More recently I read *Fix Your Life with NLP* by Alicia Eaton; it seems to have been written to address this issue of obfuscation as it is a very straightforward read and would serve well as a starter text on the subject.

I think this is a good point at which to add something about creativity, as Ian mentioned that he noticed an increase in individuals' self-esteem when participating in the creative process or, as he described it, 'a process that says there are no rights or wrongs'. During creative sessions there are no wrong answers, so let's try to sprinkle more creative opportunities throughout the curriculum. Not all the time though, as they can be exhausting even for the professionally creative, just a few here and there when the situation allows. There are a number of instant creativity activities you could employ but here's my go-to selection:

- brainstorming – great for generating ideas

- Tony Buzan's wonderful mind maps – brilliant for recording and exploring

- a creativity checklist – perfect for pushing ideas further

- mind dump – exhausting all angles of thought.

Just to touch on each briefly:

Brainstorming. Possibly a familiar idea to many people, but are you making the most of it? Ian suggests the following rules for maximum effectiveness:

- Defer judgement.

- Build on the ideas of others.

- Stay focused on the topic.

- One person at a time.

- Go for quantity (150 ideas in a 30–45 minute session).

- Encourage wild ideas.

- Be visual.

Another idea is for everyone to write down their own ideas first for a few minutes, or work in pairs to generate a list. Then the teacher can invite suggestions individually, or as a whole class. This works especially well in a school environment as everyone gets the chance to think quietly to themselves and have an idea included in the main brainstorming session, or at least see one that they had thought of even if it was said by someone else. This also works really well when each idea is written on a sticky note and then all the notes are pooled together on a large piece of paper, wall or window.

The wonderful world of mind maps. Whatever did we do before Tony Buzan? Seriously, I feel I've been using mind maps forever. If you have too, then I expect you know the mind map rules by now:

- Start in the centre of the page using an image or picture for the central topic or theme.

- Use colours and imagery as much as possible.

- Use curved lines to connect all the main branches to the centre and second and third level branches as necessary.

- Only one key word per line.

Mind maps can be used in so many ways:

Research	Seeing the whole picture	Note taking	Family trees
Learning vocabulary	Decision making	Summarising	Recording thinking
Creative writing	Project planning	Revision	Downloading thoughts

Also check out Mr Buzan's own website (www.tonybuzan.com) and his vast array of books, videos, courses and software.

A creativity checklist. I first came across this as a teenager doing a BTEC in art and design. It's a checklist you can run through to help you develop ideas for something specific. There's a *Creativity checklist* on page 111 as an example. As a teacher I used something like this extensively when helping students explore ideas for Design and Technology projects. I found it saved me from repeatedly saying: 'That's a brilliant idea to kick off with, now generate 20 more.' The look of horror I received at the mere mention of having to think up more ideas, and the energy I expended having to repeatedly point out why the first or even fourth idea wasn't necessarily the best one, caused me to generate a creativity checklist. Nifty thinking there as once students had been in a few of my classes, they were able to generate their own checklists. I encourage you to develop one for your purposes as my list may very well not suit your curriculum area. In fact, consider the following Food Technology brief: 'Create a street food that can be eaten using only hands.' Now run it through my checklist. Hilarious!

Mind dumping. First, state your problem, e.g. 'I need a revision plan I can stick to'. Then, as fast as possible so it becomes a stream of conciousness, write down 20 solutions. I'm going to do it here for real and time myself to see how long it takes me to get to 20 ideas:

I need a revision plan I can stick to	
See what my friends have done	Ask my family
Ask teachers	Use the one in school diary
Look on the internet	Pin it up big on my wall
Shrink it down so I can carry it with me	Look in the library
Ask a newspaper agony aunt	Make one into a folder
Do it as daily cards to check progress	Do a spreadsheet
Do a mind map of the weeks before my exam	Ask a doctor or an accountant

Do nothing	Sit quietly and hear what I should do
Choose a celebrity to help me	Be a celebrity when I'm revising
Make my revision area welcoming	Start in good time

So there's my thinking about revision in action and, after 30 years of creative thinking practice, I produced that lot in just under four minutes. What I love about this technique is that you can see the path I took for creative inspiration: there's plenty of 'asking others' ideas, including conjuring up a celebrity helper or two. I also thought that asking a doctor or accountant would be a good idea because their training involves lots of exams. I notice I also considered the *format* of the revision plan, as I was exploring the idea that maybe I couldn't stick to other revision plans because they weren't attractive to look at or practical to use. I can see good school advice like 'Start in good time' and 'Make my revision area welcoming' popping up too. The lovely spiritual 'Sit quietly' idea was very typical of my intuitive self and the 'Do nothing' very typical of my devil's advocate! I hope this example demonstrates how, with practice, the mind dump can actually explore all aspects of the question, not merely address the surface of a problem. By doing the exercise against the clock, you are forced to make connections and associations very quickly. Try it for yourself, then teach it to your students. Oh, and if 20 answers is too easy, up it to 50 or 100.

Another idea in this chapter about hope is to help your students create a 'Handbook for Life'. This is a kind of personal and practical scrapbook pulling together information about an individual: how they think, what their skills and talents are, what they enjoy, which over time can build up into a resource than can be useful for them to refer back to when starting new projects, progressing further in education or generally just getting by in life. It can also contain information about what they want to do with their life, where they would like to be and what gets them excited about the world. All fine and good so far but, even better, it is possible to add lots of different nuggets of information to make a Handbook for Life actually usable over and over again throughout life. Ideas might include:

- strategies for creative problem solving
- strategies for dealing with conflict and difficult people
- strategies for making decisions
- strategies for generating inspiration
- strategies for generating information
- diagrams and plans of the future
- goals and action plans
- useful snippets of information
- notes of other people's positive and constructive comments
- vision collages
- dreams and thoughts of the future
- sources of help and advice
- outcomes of decisions and reflections on actions
- advice tips.

And probably many other aspects, comments and notes, all building up into a kind of reference manual. From time to time it can be really useful to be reminded of dreams and directions in life, skills and interests that might be being neglected, practical ways to deal with difficult issues and strategies for getting out of a rut, etc.

A Handbook for Life can exist in many formats:

- notebook

- sketchbook

- portfolio sized

- pocket sized

- folder

- blog

- video/audio record

- on a computer

- as a diagram or map

- as a combination of any or all of the above.

All the things learned doing the exercises in this book, other books, other sources and resources can be collected together in this way. There is a *Handbook for life* exercise to spark some ideas on pages 115–117.

And finally, finally, if you're anything like me, you might have got to this stage in the book and be feeling a range of emotions including mild panic. If you have been inspired to try even one idea or exercise, the thought of finding the time to put it into practice in an already overloaded schedule might induce a feeling of stress. This is not the effect I want you to experience, as the aim of this book is to inspire not overwhelm. So I had a cunning plan: get others involved! If you turn to page 112, you will see a *Discussions for whole-school policies and INSET* exercise which lists all the main points in the book and gives you space to write some thoughts alongside. I'd photocopy it on to A3 paper, but then I have 'expansive' writing so I like a bit of space. Use this planner, or your version, to review how you could incorporate one, some or all of the ideas into your school, or at least your classroom. Working with two or more colleagues divides the load and doubles the thinking power!

As this last chapter draws to a close, I want to leave you with one last great story of Ian's. For me it neatly sums up much of what this book is about.

My insurance salesman left school with a CSE in technical drawing and was told by his careers teacher that, as he was good with his hands, he should go and be a bricklayer. However, rather than be any old bricklayer, my friend decided he wanted to be the best bricklayer around and that he would bricklay for England. I didn't know there was an all-England bricklaying team but there is. He won a cup and put it on the mantelpiece he had built. Then he thought to himself, 'If I can do this what else can I do?' to which the answer was, 'Own a sports car.' Not long after that he went into insurance, not because he desperately wanted to be an insurance salesman, but because he knew it would move him nearer to his goal. He was recently a member of the MDRT – the Million Dollar Round Table – a prestigious hall of fame for successful insurance professionals. Last time I met him he said that, as the government had introduced a raft of new qualifications for people in the financial world, he had a number of tricky new exams to take. He passed first time, but many of his graduate colleagues failed and had to resit. And he recently told me that he was dyslexic! If a dyslexic brickie with a CSE in technical drawing can fly this high, then what can the rest of us achieve?

And the last word goes to Henry Ford, who explained to his engineers that he wanted them to cast all four engine cylinders in one block for his new V-8 engine. Although they could do it on paper, all his engineers agreed it was actually impossible to produce. Allegedly Ford's reply was:

Do it anyway.

Creativity checklist

Apply these to your idea, plan or product and see what happens . . .

- [ ] Make it big, huge, gigantic
- [ ] Make it small, tiny, microscopic
- [ ] Divide it up into lots of little pieces
- [ ] Multiply it
- [ ] Halve it
- [ ] Make it smell better, worse, of nothing
- [ ] Make it more fun, more business-like, more heavy duty
- [ ] Reduce it to the bare essentials
- [ ] Make it rigid/pliable
- [ ] Make it smooth, knobbly, rough, slippery, heavy, delicate, intricate, unwieldy
- [ ] Make it attractive to a baby, a millionaire, someone in hospital, a celebrity
- [ ] Invert the colours
- [ ] Make it monochrome
- [ ] Turn it upside down
- [ ] Use the other hand
- [ ] Make it work backwards
- [ ] Put it online / take it offline
- [ ] Make it work in the dark / underwater / in space
- [ ] What would it say if it could speak?
- [ ] Make it from mud, electricity, cardboard, steel, cotton, jelly
- [ ] What other use could it have?
- [ ] Make it work with something that already exists
- [ ] Make it do the opposite of what you want
- [ ] See it through someone else's eyes
- [ ] What does it remind you of?
- [ ] Link it to a random word generator (see online resources)

Discussions for whole-school policies and INSET

Just in case you fancy putting this whole book into practice in your school, or feel you / the school would benefit from developing certain key themes, please put this sheet to good use and get brainstorming . . .

Chapter 1 – Motivated for what?		
Topic	**What we do now**	**How we could improve this**
Marketing subjects		
Curriculum wall		
Wish list, What makes you happy? and Design a world exercises		
Visualise your future, Capturing the dream and Make a vision board exercises		
Goal setting		
A positive attitude towards failure		

Chapter 2 – Go with the flow		
Topic	**What we do now**	**How we could improve this**
Gardner's multiple intelligences observing		
Gardner's multiple intelligences in curriculum areas		
Research and report game		
Thinking skills		
Pareto, the primacy and recency effect and mulling		
Flipping the classroom		

Chapter 3 – Mission control		
Topic	**What we do now**	**How we could improve this**
Class rules		
High challenge / low stress and Ways to get the students to generate their own learning exercise		
Play in the classroom		
Assessing teachers' own intelligences and preferences		

Chapter 4 – Get real		
Topic	**What we do now**	**How we could improve this**
Real world possibilities exercise		
Lesson planning using fartlek		
The review cycle and creating habits		
Employability score exercise		
Practising failure		
What did I do today? and Do it exercises		

Chapter 5 – Get personal		
Topic	**What we do now**	**How we could improve this**
Smiling and kindness		
Model behaviour exercise		

Topic	What we do now	How we could improve this
A healthy community exercise		
How do I feel? and I have no energy exercises		
Good habits bad habits exercise		

Chapter 6 – Reptiles in the classroom

Topic	What we do now	How we could improve this
Food and safety		
Routine, music and warm-up work		
Entertain exercise		
Positive emotions		

Chapter 7 – Motivation is a four-letter word

Topic	What we do now	How we could improve this
Giving hope and positive support		
Emotional Intelligence and self esteem		
Applying creativity		
Handbook for life		

Additional notes:

Topic	What we do now	How we could improve this

Handbook for life

Answer these questions to kick-start your Handbook for Life:

What strategies do I know for thinking about and planning my future?

What are my intelligences based on Gardner's range?

What are my favourite ways of learning new information?

What times of day do I work best?

What strategies work for me to keep my energy up?

What are the best ways for me to learn something new and remember it?

What strategies shall I use to make failure work for me?

What strategies shall I use if I am not really interested or motivated to learn something?

What people are most useful for me to model to gain extra insights?

Who are the most supportive people to have in my community?

What great habits do I want to develop?

What can I do to improve my employability score?

What are my favourite strategies for being creative?

What steps can I take to ensure I succeed in reaching my goals?

Where to start

If you've never come across activities like this or are beginning to be a bit over-whelmed with how much you still want to do with your classes, here is a suggestion of where to start implementing some of the ideas. You could start by looking at the 25 instant wins on pages 121–122, but here is a list of a rough order you might want to start putting things into practice, as I think these are where the biggest impact can be made. Just my suggestions – obviously you may already have some of these in place or feel your school/classes would benefit from a different approach. The bottom line is this: if your classes, or the whole school, had this lot going on, then things would definitely be heading in the right direction. Even implementing the first one alone could cause positive ripples that impact everyday life in your school.

- **Excitement:** Chapter 1 – Motivated for what?

  Generating a buzz about subjects can change students' attitudes and improve motivation. Even just one department, or one teacher, 'marketing' their subject in an energetic way could cause other teachers to want to do something similar, or noticeably change the dynamics of that department. The other notable positive about having excitement as the first step taken to improve motivation is that by creating the excitement you can't help being excited yourself, and who doesn't want to have excitement as an emotion associated with their workplace?

- **Class rules:** Chapter 3 – Mission control

  By implementing class rules with each of your classes, you are starting to create a safe place for your students from which they can stretch to new learning.

- **No blame culture:** Chapter 4 – Get real

  As with class rules, by exploring and even celebrating the nature of failure, an atmosphere of safety to experiment and learn is created. The no-blame culture could take some time to establish within a single class as the students may forget that your class is the special one where they can make mistakes and learn from them, as the rest of the school might be very different. A whole-school policy focused on celebrating learning by actively discussing and analysing (without apportioning blame for) mistakes would create an amazingly rich environment to learn in.

- **Music:** Chapter 6 – Reptiles in the classroom

  Easy to implement and can be used in so many different ways in the classroom, or even around the school. Using music can lift mood, aid thought, delineate learning activities, signal events and generally make the learning experience more multidimensional. Again, music in your working environment: what's not to like?

- **Breakfast club:** Chapter 6 – Reptiles in the classroom

  Well, you know my thoughts on this one. But the reason it's not the number one priority, as it rightly should be, is that (a) it might not be a major issue in your school (I hope this is the case) or (b) there is only so much you can do about student hunger. Please re-read page 93 for my suggestions as to steps to take. You can do something. And that something could change someone's life.

- **Pace:** Chapter 2 – Go with the flow

  This allows individual lessons to be less taxing for both you and your students. Pace allows an improvement in the *quality* of learning, which, in turn, allows *quantity*.

- **Goal setting:** Chapter 1 – Motivated for what?

  Without a destination the journey may well be interesting but not necessarily take you to any new places. Deliberately thinking about intangibles such as happiness and fulfilment in life and then strategically working out how to get them are valuable lifelong skills. You could even teach them to your students . . .

- **Gardner's multiple intelligences:** Chapter 2 – Go with the flow

  After many raging debates as to whether there is any value in such theories as multiple intelligences, I say 'Why not?'. Why not try them, see where students fit, see what thoughts and actions come from the explorations and evaluate accordingly? Just don't dismiss without careful thought. One of my favourite phrases in the world: what if . . .?

- **Getting out of class / getting people in:** Chapter 4 – Get real

  I'm hoping this one speaks for itself. We live in a big, challenging, scary, exciting world; why would we not want to cause external world situations to happen in school so that we can be with our students while they explore them?

- **Learning review strategy:** Chapter 4 – Get real

  Oops! It appears I've snuck in an academically based one. Well, yes, it's handy to teach your students to learn how to learn so that they can confidently tick all those exam boxes. It may also help them to confidently approach any future learning scenarios: evening classes in conversational French, how to negotiate at least 50 per cent off any given price or the operational procedures of a Mars exploration unit. You get my drift.

25 instant wins

1. Smile.

2. Act 'as if': *as if* you feel great, *as if* they're your favourite class, *as if* you have the most exciting information to impart . . .

3. Seek exisiting knowledge to attach new knowledge to.

4. Get some great entrance/exit music into your lesson.

5. Give them a sense of control, e.g. a choice of two activities and ask which they would like to do first.

6. Mental 'limbering up' at the start of a class in the form of anagrams, dingbats, small words out of a long word, etc.

7. Instant feedback in the form of on-the-spot marking, peer marking, self-marking, etc.

8. Establish a classroom routine which allows students to relax as they 'know' the framework for your lessons.

9. Add the element of novelty via suspense, intrigue, curiosity or surprise.

10. Create a Positive Wall which is an ever-changing display chock full of ideas and achievements of your students and examples of others. Encourage students to contribute.

11. Get them up, get them active, get them outside if possible.

12. When waiting for an answer, wait just a little bit longer.

13. Open a window, allow air (oxygen!) to circulate.

14. Actively encourage and support trial and error.

15. Accommodate downtime or mulling within each lesson.

16. Introduce active role-play or modelling.

17. Design your lessons as problems to be solved.

18. Introduce an element of peer teaching.

19. Find a way to stir emotions and/or engage all the senses.

20. 'Instruct' for no more than 15 minutes per hour of teaching.

21. Give your students the big picture of the elements of your curriculum subject.

22. Make an effort to discover what makes your students happy. Build it in.

23. Involve students in planning the lessons.

24. Be kind.

25. Be empathetic.

Using the worksheets

Chapter 1 – Motivated for what?	Individual	Class/ Group	Whole School	INSET
The wish list	☑			
What makes you happy?	☑	☑		☑
Design a world where anything is possible	☑	☑		
Visualise your future		☑		
Capturing the dream		☑		
Make a vision board	☑	☑	☑	☑
I can see into the future	☑	☑		
Goal setting made simple	☑	☑	☑	
Chapter 2 – Go with the flow	**Individual**	**Class/ Group**	**Whole School**	**INSET**
Gardner's intelligences quick quiz	☑	☑	☑	☑
Gardner's multiple intelligences descriptors	☑	☑	☑	☑
Who's who	☑	☑		
Brilliant intelligences activities list	☑	☑		☑
Mental workout	☑	☑		
Chapter 3 – Mission control	**Individual**	**Class/ Group**	**Whole School**	**INSET**
Class rules	☑	☑	☑	
Ways to get the students to generate their own learning	☑	☑	☑	
Research and report game	☑	☑	☑	
Chapter 4 – Get real	**Individual**	**Class/ Group**	**Whole School**	**INSET**
Real world possibilities			☑	☑
The review habit	☑	☑	☑	
Success qualities	☑	☑		
Famous failures	☑	☑		
Reflection on failure	☑	☑	☑	☑
Do it	☑	☑		☑
What did I do today?	☑	☑	☑	

Chapter 5 – Get personal	Individual	Class/ Group	Whole School	INSET
Model behaviour	☑	☑	☑	☑
A healthy community	☑	☑		
How do I feel?	☑			☑
I have no energy	☑	☑		☑
But that's boring	☑	☑	☑	
Good habits bad habits	☑	☑		☑
Chapter 6 – Reptiles in the classroom	**Individual**	**Class/ Group**	**Whole School**	**INSET**
The brain truths quiz	☑	☑		☑
Music in the classroom			☑	☑
Entertain			☑	☑
Chapter 7 – Motivation is a four-letter word	**Individual**	**Class/ Group**	**Whole School**	**INSET**
Creativity checklist	☑	☑	☑	☑
Discussions for whole-school policies and INSET				☑
Handbook for life	☑		☑	☑

Posters

The chains of habit are too light to be felt until they are too heavy to be broken.

Warren Buffet

DDM

or

DMD?

Ian Gilbert

Everybody thinks of changing humanity, and nobody thinks of changing himself.

Leo Tolstoy

Excellence is not an act but a habit.

Aristotle

Fail faster to learn quicker to succeed sooner.

Nordström and Ridderstråle
– Funky Business

Failure is simply the opportunity to begin again, this time more intelligently.

Henry Ford

Fall down seven times, get up eight.

Japanese proverb

Happiness is not a goal, it is a by-product.

Eleanor Roosevelt

Hope fires a neuron

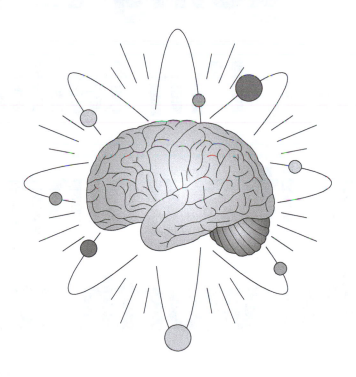

I'm not telling you it is going to be easy, I'm telling you it's going to be worth it.

Art Williams

Intelligence is what you use when you don't know what to do.

Jean Piaget

It's the thinking that goes into the writing, not the words that end up on the paper that makes the difference.

**Tom Monaghan,
founder of Domino Pizzas**

Learning

is messy.

Nobody achieved their full potential aiming for the obvious.

Ian Gilbert

Smile.
More.

Success is a lousy teacher. It seduces smart people into thinking they can't lose.

Bill Gates

Successful people are simply those with successful habits.

Brian Tracy

The world is moving so fast that the man who says it can't be done is generally interrupted by someone doing it.

Elbert Hubbard, 1915, philosopher and artist

General bibliography

Aamodt, S. and Wang, S. (2012) *Welcome to Your Child's Brain*, Oxford: Oneworld Publications

Armstrong, T. (2003) *You're Smarter Than You Think*, Minneapolis, MN: Free Spirit Publishing Inc.

Beadle, P. (2010) *How to Teach*, Carmarthen: Crown House Publishing

Buzan, T. (2003) *Brain Child*, London: Harper Collins

Claxton, G. (2008) *What's the Point of School?*, Oxford: Oneworld Publications

Claxton, G., Chambers, M., Powell, G. and Lucas, B. (2011) *The Learning Powered School*, Bristol: TLO Limited

Duhigg, C. (2013) *The Power of Habit*, London: Random House

Dweck, C. (2012) *Mindset*, London: Constable & Robinson Ltd

Eaton, A. (2012) *Fix Your Life with NLP*, London: Simon & Schuster

Facer, K. (2011) *Learning Futures*, Abingdon: Routledge

Gallo, C. (2014) *Talk like TED*, London: Macmillan

Gerver, R. (2010) *Creating Tomorrow's Schools Today*, London: Continuum

Ginnins, P. (2002) *The Teacher's Toolkit*, Carmarthen: Crown House Publishing

Grant Halvorson, H. (2012) *9 Things Successful People Do Differently*, Boston, MA: Harvard Business School Publishing Corporation

Griffith, A. and Burns, M. (2012) *Engaging Learners*, Carmarthen: Crown House Publishing

Hardy, D. (2010) *The Compound Effect*, New York: Vanguard Press

Keller, G with Papasan, J. (2013) *The One Thing*, London: John Murray

Knight, O. and Benson, D. (2014) *Creating Outstanding Classrooms*, Abingdon: Routledge

Koch, R. (2007) *The 80/20 Principle*, London: Nicholas Brealey Publishing

Ryan, W. (2011) *Inspirational Teachers, Inspirational Learners*, Carmarthen: Crown House Publishing

Smith, P. (2012) *Lead with a Story*, New York: American Management Association

Strang, J., Masterson, P. and Button, O. (2007) *ASK: How to Teach Learning-to-Learn in Secondary Schools*, Carmarthen: Crown House Publishing

Swann, M., Peacock, A., Hart, S. and Drummond, M, (2012) *Creating Learning without Limits*, Maidenhead: Open University Press

Tokuhama-Espinosa, T. (2014) *Making Classrooms Better*, New York: W.W. Norton & Company, Inc.

Willingham, D. (2009) *Why Don't Students Like School?*, San Francisco, CA: Jossey-Bass

Index

Please note the page numbers in bold indicate the actual page where the exercise can be found.